# Washington

## Local and Seasonal
# Cookbook

Becky Selengut
Jennifer Sayers Bajger
James Darcy
with contributions from
Jennifer Ogle

LONE PINE

Lone Pine Publishing International

**Distributed by Lone Pine Publishing**
1808 B Street NW, Suite 140
Auburn, WA, USA  98001

Website: www.lonepinepublishing.com

Publisher's Cataloging-In-Publication Data
(Prepared by The Donohue Group, Inc.)


Selengut, Becky.
   The Washington local and seasonal cookbook / Becky Selengut, Jennifer Sayers Bajger, James Darcy ; with contributions from Jennifer Ogle.

   p. : ill. ; cm.

   Includes index.
   ISBN-13: 978-976-8200-46-4
   ISBN-10: 976-8200-46-4

   1. Cookery, American—Pacific Northwest style. 2. Cookery—Washington (State) I. Bajger, Jennifer Sayers. II. Darcy, James W., 1976- III. Ogle, Jennifer. IV. Title.

TX715.2.P32 S45 2007
641.59797

Front cover photography by Nanette Samol and photos.com.

*Photography:* All photographs by Nanette Samol, except those on p. 18, 22, 54, 62, 66, 68, 70, 72, 94, 116, 122, 132, 146, 154, 160, 164, 184 and 186 by Merle Prosofsky.
*Prop Credits:* Pnina Staav, Le Gnome.

Special thanks to Lovoni Walker for her recipe and food styling for Smoked Salmon and Asparagus Salad, p. 14.


*PC:* 15

# CONTENTS

## DEDICATION

This book is dedicated to the incredible farmers, fishermen and artisan producers of Washington state. They allow us to enjoy our lives one bite at a time.

For Gummy—bls

# INTRODUCTION

Washington state captivates the hearts—and stomachs—of both locals and travelers alike, and for good reason. Few places in the world are home to island, sea and verdant woods on one side of the state and desert, vineyards and orchards on the other. It is precisely this diversity of climate that fosters a profusion of such varied local foods. The Cascade Mountains divide the two sides of our state, casting a rainshadow and temperate weather over western Washington while eastern Washington bakes under the warmth of the sun. Our state offers visitors and inhabitants whole worlds of food possibilities.

We are blessed with abundant farmland, the vast waters of the Pacific Ocean and its resident native salmon, pristine inland lakes and streams, and miles of hiking trails along which grow wild mushrooms, huckleberries and edible greens. With a little knowledge and a good map, a traveler in our state could eat very well indeed, without *ever* setting foot in a supermarket.

Local farms and ranches bring us grass-fed meats, free-range eggs, organic vegetables, fruits and grains. Artisan and small producers offer almost every imaginable food—from farmstead cheeses, microbrewed beer, world class wine and hand-crafted bread, to preserves, ice cream and pies—all made from locally grown ingredients.

Food is a vital part of history and culture. It reflects a place and the people who live there. Washington's food producers have a rich history that ties their origins with their present places to create a unique and diverse culture. People from all over the world have settled in Washington and brought their traditional foods with them, enriching our state with new recipes adapted to the available bounty.

In the past, if a food wasn't in season, we probably couldn't get it. The foods we ate changed depending on the time of the year, and we had an intimate connection with our food and where it came from. Now, fresh food can quickly travel from around the world to our dinner tables. Wide selection and convenience are the great advantages of our modern world. The great disadvantage is that we have become disconnected from where our food comes from. We give little thought to how far it has had to travel and what financial, ethical or environmental costs the production of imported food may have.

Eating seasonally takes advantage of what locally grown foods are available. It supports the local economy, and it often provides us with fresher and tastier food. Perhaps most importantly, it connects us to the origins of our food. By speaking directly to food producers at such places as farmers' markets, U-pick farms and wineries, we learn not only of the spectrum of foods available at home, but the value of the people involved in their production. We can even become food producers ourselves, by growing our own fruits or vegetables in our gardens or balcony planters.

Eating with the seasons requires a bit of discipline. First, we need to educate ourselves about what thrives in our environment and when it comes into season. Then, we need to know how to use that knowledge to change the way we put food on the table. With a bit of investment, we can reap tremendous rewards. Soon, we know that summer has fully arrived not just because of the calendar and the feeling of the sun on our faces but by the tomato, eggplant, peppers and corn spilling over the farmer's market tables. The passage of fall into winter is marked by chanterelles and squash waxing and then waning, edging us towards hearty braised meats, cheeses and wine. When the rains abate, spring emerges with chartreuse profusions of peas and asparagus, and earthy brown morels. Then, it begins all over again.

In time, the thought of a tomato in February, flown in from Argentina in the dead of winter, suddenly feels totally wrong. After all, is it really a deprivation to not eat a red, mealy tomato that is a wisp of its true self? What at first might feel like a hardship (*no* fresh tomatoes *all* winter long?) transitions into the best gift you could ever give yourself and your loved ones. Not only is eating seasonally better for the environment, your local economy and your health, it is simply better for your taste buds.

With this book, we have created a resource of recipes that represent some of the best of what Washington has to offer. We have tried to capture a slice of the food, recipes, producers and culture that makes us unique. Perhaps we're biased in saying that when you sample our foods, lovingly transformed from producer through the hands of a cook who truly appreciates the ingredients, you are tasting the best we have to offer. We wouldn't have it any other way.

# In Our Kitchen

We have found the following ingredient choices and cooking procedures to be successful in our kitchen and recommend them highly wherever possible.

Butter is unsalted and is easiest to measure using the convenient markings on the wrapping.

Citrus juices are fresh squeezed.

Eggs are large, free-range eggs. They should be at room temperature for baking.

Flour is unbleached all-purpose.

Herbs are fresh, unless stated otherwise. In a pinch, the best alternative to fresh is frozen. You can freeze herbs yourself in the summer when they are plentiful, and you can even find them in the freezer section of some of the better grocery stores.

Mushrooms, such as morels and chanterelles, can be found in the wild, but we advise that you confirm the identification of mushrooms with an experienced collector before cooking them; some species are acutely toxic and can cause death.

Stocks are homemade. Good quality stocks in cans or asceptic boxes are the best substitute. Avoid using those nasty little cubes. Miso, a fermented soybean paste, is another interesting alternative to stock, and it will keep in the refrigerator for several months. Stir it in 1 Tbsp at a time until you have a rich, full flavor.

Sugar is organic and unrefined rather than white and bleached. When looking for a rich brown sugar, use muscovado sugar, available in grocery and health food stores. It retains the minerals and vitamins originally in the sugar cane plant, and it has a full molasses flavor.

Yeast is regular dry yeast; ½ oz dry yeast is equal to 1 Tbsp fresh yeast.

# Measuring

Dry ingredients should be spooned into the measuring cup and leveled off with a knife or spatula.

Solids, including butter and most cheeses, are measured in dry-measure cups and liquids in liquid-measure cups.

# Essential Ingredients

The following ingredients are used in many of the recipes in this book; special ingredients found in just one or two recipes are described where they are used. Some items are widely available, whereas others are best sought in gourmet, specialty food, health food or ethnic stores or obtained by mail order or the Internet.

**Bay Leaves**— Fresh leaves have such a different flavor that they are worth the effort to find. They are occasionally available at large grocery stores and can be specially ordered. In a well-sealed container in the fridge, they can last three or four months.

**Coconut Milk**—Use unsweetened coconut milk in cans. Naturally sweet, it is often better than cream in savory dishes.

**Garlic**—Use fresh garlic! An Italian friend says that if you can't be bothered to peel and chop fresh garlic you shouldn't be allowed to use it!

**Lemons and Limes**—Use fresh! You can't compare the taste to concentrate.

**Mayonnaise**—It's always better homemade:

**5 egg yolks**

**⅔ cup extra virgin olive oil**

**¼ cup good quality vinegar or juice from 1 lemon**

**pinch of sea salt to taste**

- You need both hands free to make mayonnaise. Spread a damp cloth on your counter, nestle a medium-sized bowl in its center and wrap it around the base of the bowl to keep it steady while you whisk.

- Whisk yolk, vinegar and salt in bowl until well combined and yolk has lightened in color.

- Add oil, a drop at a time, whisking continuously until mixture emulsifies and thickens.

- When about half of oil has been added, whisk in remaining oil in a slow, steady stream. Store, covered, in refrigerator for up to five days. You can thin your mayonnaise by lightly whisking in some water.

- Many people like to add mustard or fresh herbs to their mayonnaise. Adding minced garlic turns plain mayonnaise into aioli. Makes just over 1 cup.

**Mustard**—Use good quality mustard for everything from sandwiches to dressings to sauces. When you are down to the last few teaspoons clinging to the bottom and sides of your mustard jar, add fresh lemon juice, olive oil, sea salt and fresh pepper for a yummy impromptu salad dressing. Just shake and enjoy.

**Oil, Sesame**—Use for a nutty flavor addition. Store it in the fridge.

**Oil, Olive**—Extra virgin olive oil is indispensable. Try olive oil from Italy, Spain or Greece.

**Oil, Grape Seed**—Use for higher heat cooking.

**Pepper, Fresh**—Freshly ground pepper has a far superior flavor to pre-ground, which loses a lot of its pungency and spice. A variety of peppercorns are available. Black or white pepper can be used interchangeably in any of the recipes, although their flavor is slightly different.

**Peppers**—When handling hot peppers, wear plastic or rubber gloves to avoid capsaicin burns. Capsaicin is the compound in all varieties of pepper (except bell peppers) that gives them their heat, and it is easily transferred through skin-to-skin contact. If you decide to live dangerously and forego the gloves, make sure you wash your hands thoroughly before touching your face, eyes or loved ones.

**Salt**—Great salt is the key to great cooking. Salt brings out the flavor in food. There are many amazing salts in the world to reach for—sea salt, kosher salt or flavored salts—choose a favorite. Better yet, obtain some of each. Before you reach for that can of Morton's, remember that it can have a chemical aftertaste, and using a better quality salt also means that you will use less, because the flavor is more intense. If you need to reduce salt even further for health reasons, use fresh herbs, various spices and flavor lifters such as lemon juice to maintain the intensity while reducing the salt content.

**Soy Sauce**—Both tamari and shoyu are high quality, fermented and chemical-free sauces that are used to enhance flavor and impart a unique saltiness.

**Star Anise**—This strongly anise-scented Oriental spice is commonly sold dried, as quarter-sized, star-shaped clusters of 5 to 10 pods, each containing a single seed. The seeds can be used on their own, crushed or ground, or the entire stars can be added, then removed.

**Vinegar, Apple Cider**—Use when you need an all-purpose vinegar; organic, unrefined and unpasteurized apple cider vinegar has the best flavor.

**Vinegar, Balsamic**—Balsamic vinegar is an aged reduction sauce that originates in the Modena region of Italy. It adds a deep, rich yet piquant, flavor to everything from soups to sweets. White balsamic vinegar is a pale gold variation that is not caramelized during processing and is not aged as long as regular balsamic vinegar. It is used in salads but can also be used in pale sauces served with a variety of meats, poultry and seafood.

SPRING

SUMMER

FALL

WINTER

# Asparagus and Quillisascut Goat Cheese Salad

### Serves 4

Washington state is rapidly becoming a haven for lovers of farmstead cheeses. A pioneer in this region is the Quillisascut Goat Cheese Company, started in 1987 and located in the small town of Rice in the northeast part of the state not too far from the beautiful Columbia River. Quillisascut is run by the affable duo Lora Lea and Rick Misterly. This energetic couple has made their mark in Washington not only with their delicious goat cheeses, but also with their ground-breaking Farm School for the Domestic Arts, which trains chefs, culinary students and the interested public. Besides learning the daily routine of farm life, including butchering chickens and milking goats, Quillisascut's students develop a tremendous appreciation for the source of their ingredients and the importance of preserving ties to local producers.

**1 x 2 lb bunch of asparagus, trimmed**

**splash of olive oil**

**sea salt and freshly ground pepper to taste**

**1 lb package of frozen peas, refreshed in boiling water, drained and cooled**

**1 cup crumbled goat cheese**

**½ cup chopped fresh mint**

**½ cup chopped fresh basil**

**1 lime, cut into 4 wedges**

Preheat barbecue to medium-high. Toss trimmed asparagus with olive oil, salt and pepper. Grill for 4 minutes, turning once. Set aside.

In a bowl, toss together the remaining ingredients, except the lime. Cut the warm asparagus into bite-sized pieces and add to the bowl. Toss and season again if needed. (You cut the asparagus after cooking because it is much easier to grill if left whole!) Divide among 4 plates and garnish each salad with a lime wedge.

**Tip**
Soft cheeses such as goat cheeses do not slice well—they often end up as a crumbled mess, half stuck to the knife. The easiest way to cut soft cheese is with taut dental floss—just make sure it's unflavored floss!

**Tip**
Allow cheese to come to room temperature for at least 30 minutes (longer for hard cheese or if the room is particularly cold) before serving in order to enjoy its full flavor and aroma. Portion cheese, if desired, while cold and keep it wrapped so it doesn't dry out before you are ready to serve.

# Pea Shoot and Enoki Mushroom Salad

### Serves 4 to 6

Every spring in western Washington, green-thumbed home cooks anxiously await the arrival of the first shoots from their pea plants. If they're lucky, the trimmings from the initial growth of pea plants yield whimsical curly tendrils and perhaps even a pea blossom—deliciously sweet, the blossom is a delicacy all on its own. Snow peas are often cultivated commercially just for their shoots; with a long tradition in Chinese cuisine, they are called "dau miu" in Cantonese. If gathered young enough, the shoots are delicious raw. If they are a bit tough, just put them in a hot pan with a little oil for a few minutes to refresh their tender deliciousness.

**Miso-Ginger Dressing**
⅓ **cup rice vinegar**

2 Tbsp white or yellow
miso paste

2 Tbsp minced pickled ginger

1 Tbsp brown sugar

1 Tbsp light soy sauce

¼ cup peanut or
grape seed oil

2 tsp sesame oil

**Salad**
4 cups pea shoots

1½ cups enoki mushrooms,
bases trimmed, mushrooms
separated

1 cup daikon radish, cut into
ribbons with a vegetable
peeler

2 Tbsp each black and white
sesame seeds

Place vinegar, miso paste, pickled ginger, brown sugar and soy sauce in blender. Purée until smooth. With blender still running, slowly drizzle in both oils.

Mix pea shoots, mushrooms and radish in a large bowl. Toss with dressing and sesame seeds.

Divide among 4 to 6 salad plates and serve.

*Enoki mushrooms, also known as "velvet foot" mushrooms, have a delicate flavor and, when eaten raw, a pleasant crunch. If you cook them, add them at the end of cooking time to preserve their flavor and texture.*

Peas are legumes and, like most legumes, have special nodules on their roots that enable them to take nitrogen from the air and return it to the soil. This function actually allows the peas to enrich the soil they grow in.

# Smoked Salmon and Asparagus Salad

## Serves 4

This incredibly delicious salad offers the opportunity to use many amazing Washington products, including fresh asparagus, cranberries, honey and—most importantly—smoked salmon! This West Coast delicacy is generally at the top of the list of items visitors like to take back home with them. This recipe uses cold smoked salmon, or lox, as it is sometimes called, which is salmon that is cured but not cooked, so it has a unique flavor and texture. Smoked salmon is also available hot smoked and made into jerky or smoked salmon candy. If you're not already familiar with some of these products, make sure you try them the next time you are at your local fish counter.

¼ cup coarsely chopped, dried sweetened cranberries

1 Tbsp drained and chopped capers

2 tsp honey

2 tsp balsamic vinegar

1 clove garlic, minced

2 Tbsp olive oil

sea salt and freshly ground pepper

1 x 2 lb bunch of asparagus, trimmed

5 oz cold smoked salmon slices

⅓ cup crème fraîche

1 large ripe avocado, peeled and sliced

chives and dill for garnish

Combine cranberries, capers, honey, vinegar, garlic, oil and salt and pepper in a small saucepan. Stir over medium heat until warm. Let stand for 15 minutes to allow cranberries to soften.

Blanch asparagus in a large saucepan of boiling, salted water for about 2 minutes or until bright green; drain. Immediately place asparagus in a bowl of iced water. Let stand about 10 minutes or until cool; drain. Return asparagus to same bowl. Add cranberry dressing and toss to combine.

Arrange asparagus on 4 serving plates; drizzle with dressing. Top with smoked salmon, some crème fraîche, avocado, more crème fraîche and smoked salmon. Garnish with chives and dill if desired.

### Tip
If you can't find crème fraîche, use sour cream instead.

*Spring, coho and sockeye salmon have a higher fat content than other species of salmon, and so have the best flavor when smoked.*

# Carmelized Onion and Asiago Stuffed Morels

### Serves 4 as an appetizer

Morel mushrooms are highly coveted by Washington chefs. Known for their nut-like flavor and meaty texture, morels grow year after year on the same forested sites. They prefer the company of pines and firs, but they flourish in the years immediately following a forest fire. In lower elevations, start looking for morels in late April and early May; as the season progresses, start looking higher up. When stuffed with sweet, caramelized onions and salty Italian cheese, these mushrooms make a perfect appetizer.

1 Tbsp grape seed or canola oil

½ cup diced white onion

1 lb fresh morels; reserve 12 of the largest to stuff, and chop the rest

¼ cup white wine

1 clove garlic, minced

¼ cup chopped parsley

2 Tbsp chopped chives

¼ cup grated Asiago cheese

2 to 3 Tbsp panko (see p. 69)

sea salt and freshly ground pepper to taste

In a medium saucepan, heat the oil over medium heat and sauté the onions until they start to caramelize, about 5 minutes. Add the chopped mushrooms and white wine, and cook for about 5 minutes. Add garlic, cook for 2 to 3 minutes and remove pan from heat. Stir in remaining ingredients, except for the 12 reserved morels. Stuff the reserved mushrooms with the filling.

**Tip**
To remove any unwanted critters hiding in the morels, soak mushrooms in salted water for at least 1 hour.

### Breading

Place flour, eggs and panko into separate shallow bowls. Place clarified butter in a saucepan over medium-high heat. Bread the stuffed )morels one at a time, dipping first in the flour, then the egg and finally the panko. Cook the mushrooms in the butter until brown and crispy. Serve hot with Lime Mayonnaise.

½ cup flour

3 eggs, lightly beaten

2 cups panko (see p. 69)

1 cup clarified butter (see Tip)

### Lime Mayonnaise

Stir together the zest from 1 lime and ½ cup mayonnaise (see p. 7) and set aside.

### Tip

To make clarified butter, melt unsalted butter slowly over low heat. Gradually, froth will rise to the top over a layer of clear golden oil in the middle and a layer of milk solids on the bottom. Clarified butter is the middle layer. Skim off the froth and carefully ladle out the clear oil, leaving out the milk solids.

# Pickled Sea Beans

**Makes approximately 4 x 8-oz jars**

"Half-way down hangs one who gathers samphire; dreadful trade"—that's what Shakespeare wrote in *King Lear*. He was describing his fellow countrymen hanging precariously on the cliffs of Dover, gathering the delicate, crisp, ocean-licked maritime specialty known as rock samphire *(Crithmum maritimum)*. Often called "sea beans," the samphires found in North America (*Salicornia* species; also known as saltwort, pickleweed or sea asparagus) are more conveniently gathered from salt marshes or sheltered beaches and tidal flats. Coastal Natives ate sea beans as a vegetable. European settlers enjoyed them pickled, and pickling is still the most common method of preparation. Sea beans are increasingly popular and are becoming readily available in restaurants. You can enjoy them as a fresh vegetable or even sautéed with a bit of garlic, but blanch them briefly in boiling water first to draw out some of their saltiness.

1½ lbs fresh sea beans

garlic cloves, peeled (optional)

1½ cups water

½ cup white balsamic vinegar (see p. 8)

⅔ cup sugar

2 Tbsp kosher salt

1 tsp mustard seeds

1 Tbsp pink peppercorns

½ tsp minced fresh ginger

Blanch sea beans in boiling water for 5 to 10 seconds, then plunge into ice water to help leach out some saltiness. Pack drained beans into sterilized jars and add a few cloves of garlic to each, if desired. Bring remaining ingredients to a boil, and simmer for 15 minutes. Allow liquid to cool to room temperature, then pour over beans. Marinate in refrigerator at least 24 hours before serving.

**Tip**
Pickled sea beans will keep for 1 month, refrigerated.

**Tip**
To sterilize jars, fill washed jars with
hot (not boiling) water. Place on a
rack in a water-filled pot. The water
level should be at least 1 inch higher
than the jar rims. Bring to a boil.
Boil for 10 minutes (at sea level—
add 1 minute for each 1000 feet
of altitude).

# Cider-roasted Pacific Oysters

**Serves 6 to 8 as an appetizer**

Oysters are one of the Pacific Northwest's culinary hallmarks. They are a pleasure to eat raw on the half shell or cooked as in this delicious recipe on the grill.
Five different types of oysters are cultivated in Washington waters: Pacific,
European Flat, Olympia (native to the area), Kumamoto and Eastern (also known
as Virginica). This recipe is a perfect showcase for the larger Pacific oyster and
is an excellent way to introduce a novice to the wonderful world of succulent,
sweet, briny oysters. Look for the following local varieties: Willapa Bay, Penn
Cove, Quilcene and Dabob Bay.

**1 Tbsp butter**

**3 Tbsp minced shallots**

**¾ cup apple or pear cider**

**2 Tbsp grainy Dijon
mustard**

**1 Tbsp chopped fresh
thyme**

**1 tsp chopped capers**

**sea salt and freshly ground
pepper**

**24 fresh oysters**

Melt butter in a small saucepan over medium-low
heat. Stir in shallots and cook about 1 minute,
until fragrant. Pour cider into pan and cook until
slightly reduced, about 10 minutes. Remove from
heat and stir in mustard, thyme and capers to
blend. Season to taste with salt and pepper.

Remove the oysters from their shells. Rinse
oysters and shells separately under cold running
water. Drain well. Place each oyster in a cupped
half shell and spoon sauce overtop. Put oyster
shells directly on the grill over medium-
high heat. Grill about 3 to 5 minutes until the edges of the oysters start to curl.

Arrange shells on platters
and allow guests to help
themselves, or divide
among 6 to 8 small
plates.

**Tip**
Cooking the oysters this way will infuse them with the flavors of the sauce all the way through the meat. If you are short on time, or anxious to eat, skip opening the oysters ahead of time. Instead, put them straight onto the grill and they'll steam open (oysters that do not open should be discarded). Remove the flat shell and spoon the sauce onto each oyster just before serving.

*To shuck oysters, scrub them with a stiff-bristled brush. With a towel folded in the palm of your hand, hold an oyster firmly with the cupped side facing down. Use an oyster knife to pry the shell open and detach the top shell. Scrape the oyster from the bottom shell. (Or ask your fishmonger to shuck the oysters for you if you're going to eat them the same day.)*

# Clam Chowder and Tea-smoked Scallops

## Serves 6

This recipe is inspired by traditional New England clam chowder but uses the best of Pacific Northwest seafood to make it our own. Pick up some fresh manila or littleneck clams (or look for fresh local razor clams in the spring and summer or get them frozen year-round) along with some wild weathervane scallops for this creamy soup. The scallops are sustainably harvested from Alaska and are occasionally available from Oregon. Washington is a world leader in clam production. Over 85 million pounds of shellfish are raised annually, contributing an estimated $110 million a year to the region's economy. Thousands of family-wage jobs in coastal communities are provided by this significant industry.

### Clams

2 cups white wine

2 cloves garlic, minced

sea salt and freshly ground pepper

4 lbs hard-shelled clams, well scrubbed

### Scallops

2 Tbsp sugar

2 Tbsp rice

¼ cup oolong loose tea

6 scallops, shucked

olive oil for brushing scallops

In a large pot, bring wine and garlic to a boil, season lightly with salt and pepper, add clams and cook until they open, about 5 minutes. Discard any that do not open. Transfer remaining clams to a bowl. Reserve liquid (clam nectar), straining with a fine mesh colander.

Line a wide pot with foil (to save your pot and make clean-up a snap). Sprinkle sugar, rice and tea on foil. Brush both sides of scallops lightly with oil. Place a wire rack, such as a small cooling rack, in pot and position scallops on rack so that they do not touch. Turn heat to high. When tea starts to smoke, cover pot tightly and reduce heat to low. Cook for 4 to 5 minutes. Turn off heat and let scallops rest an additional 2 to 3 minutes.

*Geoducks are big business in the south Puget Sound. They are the world's largest clam and can sometimes fetch equally large prices on the world market. They are enjoyed locally as sashimi in Seattle's top sushi restaurants, sliced and added to chowder, or made into fritters. Just the act of saying geoduck (pronounced "gooey-duck") can peg you as a local or a tourist. "Oyster Bill" Whitbeck at Taylor Shellfish Farm is a great source for farmed geoduck.*

## Chowder

In a heavy pot, sauté onions in butter and oil until golden. Add vegetables, bay leaf and reserved clam nectar, and cover with stock. Simmer for 15 minutes, then add clams and cream. Simmer for 10 to 15 minutes more or until potatoes are cooked and soup is reduced and creamy. Ladle soup into individual bowls, and garnish each with a scallop and sprinkle of herbs.

## Tip

For best results, time the scallops and chowder to be ready at the same time.

You can substitute ½ cup diced bacon, cooked until crispy, for the scallops. You could also dice the scallops and stir them into the soup.

**2 medium onions, diced**

**¼ cup unsalted butter**

**1 Tbsp olive oil**

**2 cups diced celery**

**1 cup diced carrots**

**3 medium potatoes, peeled and diced**

**1 bay leaf**

**reserved clam nectar**

**fish or clam stock, enough to just cover vegetables**

**clams, as prepared opposite**

**2 cups heavy cream (32 percent)**

**scallops, as prepared opposite**

**¼ cup fresh herbs, such as parsley, thyme or tarragon**

# Dunlop Farms Lamb with Mustard Spaetzle

### Serves 4

Lopez Island is located in the San Juan Islands, which prides itself on its 247 days of sunshine and half the rainfall of Seattle, its big city neighbor to the southeast. All that sun with still a fair amount of rain allows for perfect pasture for Bruce Dunlop to raise his lamb. Dunlop's lamb is not only delicious, but its lifelong grass diet leads to meat rich in omega-3 fatty acids and antioxidants, and it is naturally leaner than animals raised or finished on grain.

**2 x 1½ lb lamb racks, frenched (trimmed and ready to use; available in most grocery stores)**

**2 Tbsp extra virgin olive oil**

**sea salt and freshly ground pepper**

**1 clove garlic, minced**

**1 cup chopped fresh parsley**

**2 Tbsp each chopped fresh thyme and rosemary**

**¼ cup breadcrumbs**

**¼ cup Dijon mustard**

**Spaetzle**

**1¼ cups flour**

**1 tsp sea salt**

**3 large eggs**

**⅓ cup milk**

**1 Tbsp grainy Dijon mustard**

Place a heavy-bottomed pan over medium-high heat. Brush lamb with oil and season with salt and pepper. Sear lamb until brown on all sides. Remove from heat and let sit 15 minutes.

Preheat oven to 450° F. Mix garlic and herbs together in a bowl with breadcrumbs. Place lamb on a small, rimmed baking sheet; brush Dijon mustard on rounded side of lamb. Divide bread-crumb mixture evenly over mustard to form a crust. Bake for 10 to 15 minutes or until a thermometer inserted in center reaches 140° F for medium rare. Let rest 5 to 10 minutes before cutting into chops.

For the spaetzle, bring a large pot of salted water to a boil. Set a bowl of ice water near pot. Sift flour and salt together. Whisk together eggs, milk and Dijon mustard and pour into flour, stirring to make a smooth batter. Using a spaetzle maker or food mill, drop batter into boiling water. When spaetzle come to surface, transfer them to ice water with a slotted spoon. Repeat until all batter is used. As they cool, remove spaetzle from water and place in sieve to drain. To reheat spaetzle, toss them in hot butter or sauce—or fry them over medium heat until golden.

Spaetzle or spätzle ("little sparrow") are dumplings very similar to pasta. They are served as a side dish and are common fare, especially in southern Germany and the Alsace region. Spaetzle makers are available at specialty food shops, department stores and German markets (where you will likely find a good one for a reasonable price).

# Green Curry Halibut

## Serves 4

There are many ways to tell it's spring in Washington state, beginning with the smell in the air as the soil heats up and the spring rains bring a profusion of crocuses and daffodils. Another sign? Local fishmarkets fill up with gorgeous, gigantic fillets of the first spring catch of Pacific halibut. At its best from mid-March to mid-November, halibut can weigh up to 700 pounds and can grow to 9 feet long. Halibut has a mild flavor, but holds its own with the complex flavors in this green curry. While enjoying your dinner, you can also feel good that the halibut fishery is so well regulated it is rated a "best choice" by the Monterey Bay Aquarium's Seafood Watch program. Not only is halibut a sustainable choice, it is also locally significant—the U.S. commercial fishery started in 1888, when halibut were first landed in Tacoma.

**Green Curry Paste**

2 fresh green chiles, seeded and chopped

2 scallions, white and green parts, chopped

1 small shallot, minced

1 clove garlic, crushed

1 stem lemongrass, white part only, chopped

1 Tbsp grape seed oil

½ Tbsp chopped fresh coriander root

3 whole green peppercorns

3 tsp fresh chopped cilantro

1 tsp ground cumin

1 tsp finely grated lime zest

1 tsp shrimp paste

½ tsp ground coriander

½ tsp ground turmeric

½ tsp sea salt

Combine all the green curry paste ingredients in a food processor or blender and purée until smooth.

Heat oil in a deep sauté pan over low heat. Add the curry paste and cook 1 to 2 minutes, until fragrant. Stir in coconut milk, kaffir lime leaves, galangal and fish sauce, and mix well.

Turn heat up to medium and bring to a boil. Add halibut to the pan and simmer, uncovered, for 15 minutes, until tender. Stir in cilantro. Serve over rice.

**Tip**
You'll need to visit an Asian grocer to find some of the ingredients for this dish.

**Halibut**

1 Tbsp grape seed or olive oil

2½ cups coconut milk

2 kaffir lime leaves

¾ of a piece dried galangal root

1 Tbsp fish sauce

1 lb skinless halibut fillet, cut into 2-inch cubes or chunks

3 Tbsp chopped cilantro

# Gnocchi in a Sorrel Sauce

### Serves 2 as a main course, 4 as a side dish

Gnocchi, which means "dumplings" in Italian, are one of the most versatile Italian dishes. Commonly made using potatoes and semolina flour, these little balls should be as light as air. They work well with a variety of sauces, including this tasty sorrel sauce. But also try variations, including creamy blue cheese, truffles or even just a simple meat sauce. The secret to gnocchi is not to overcook them because they will start to fall apart. As with all Italian pasta dishes, *al dente*, or "tender to the tooth," is the desired doneness!

½ recipe gnocchi (see opposite) or 1 lb package of gnocchi

splash of olive oil

1 Tbsp unsalted butter

1 small shallot, minced

½ cup white wine

1 cup heavy cream (32 percent)

1 packed cup chopped sorrel

¼ cup chopped parsley

sea salt and freshly ground pepper to taste

good sized pinch of chopped fresh chives

handful of freshly grated Parmesan cheese

Bring a big pot of salted water to a rolling boil and cook the gnocchi until they float to the surface. Drain, toss with a splash of olive oil and set aside.

In a large saucepan, heat the butter and add the shallot and cook for 2 to 3 minutes, then add the white wine and cook until the wine has reduced by half. Add the cream and continue cooking for 5 minutes at medium-high.

Purée sorrel and parsley in a blender along with hot cream mixture until everything is incorporated; the sauce turns jade green in color. Pour sauce back into pan along with the gnocchi just to heat through, and season with salt and pepper. Serve in warm bowls with chives and Parmesan cheese sprinkled on top.

## Gnocchi

Preheat oven to 350° F. Pierce potatoes with a fork in several places. Bake on a baking sheet until tender, about 45 minutes to an hour, flipping halfway through. Remove from oven and peel as soon as possible (use an oven mitt or tea towel to protect your hand). Pass the potatoes through a ricer or food mill. Spread the potato out in an even layer on your cutting board and let cool for 15 minutes.

2 lbs baking potatoes
(2 large russets)

1 egg, lightly beaten

1 cup all-purpose flour

pinch of nutmeg

pinch of fine grain sea salt

In a medium bowl, mix nutmeg and salt into flour. Pull the potato into a mound. Pour the beaten egg overtop, then sprinkle ¾ cup of the flour over that. Use a spatula to scrape up some of the dough and fold it over, repeating until the egg and flour are just incorporated throughout the potato. Knead briefly and gently, adding the remaining flour a sprinkle at a time if the dough seems too sticky.

Cut dough into 8 pieces, and roll each piece into a rope as thick as your thumb. With a knife, cut each rope into ¾-inch pieces. Take a fork in one hand, and roll each gnocchi down the length of the fork.

Use half the gnocchi to make the recipe at left; dust the other half with flour and freeze on a baking sheet before transferring to a freezer bag to keep up to 6 months in the freezer.

# Spring Vegetable Risotto with Fava Beans, Morels and Pea Vines

**Serves 4**

Risotto is a traditional Italian dish that you can find in many of the state's finest restaurants (and not just Italian ones). This method of cooking rice uses a special variety of rice called Arborio (Carnaroli or Vialone Nano can also be used), which is "toasted" or sautéed in olive oil or butter before broth is added to the pan. The result is a very creamy rice that has a nice *al dente* bite to it when it has finished cooking. Risotto is infinitely adaptable, changing along with the seasons. In spring, morels start to pop up in the mountains; searching for them with someone skilled in mushroom identification is a quintessential Pacific Northwest experience. The addition of fava beans, known in Italian as *carne di poveri* or "poor man's meat" owing to their high protein content, adds a slightly nutty, buttery and vibrant green-ness to the risotto that surely heralds the coming of spring.

**4 cups vegetable or chicken broth**

**2 Tbsp olive oil, divided**

**2 Tbsp butter, divided**

**6 oz fresh morel mushrooms, cleaned and sliced**

**½ lb fava beans, shelled**

**1 small onion, finely chopped**

**1 clove garlic, minced**

**1 cup Arborio or Carnaroli rice**

**½ cup dry white wine**

**1 cup fresh pea vines, plus a few more for garnish**

**⅓ cup freshly grated Parmesan cheese**

**sea salt and freshly ground pepper to taste**

In a medium saucepan, bring broth nearly to a boil, then reduce heat to low to keep warm.

In a large sauté pan, melt 1 Tbsp olive oil and 1 Tbsp butter over medium-low heat. Add morels and cook until tender, about 3 to 5 minutes. Add favas and cook until warmed through, another minute or two. Season with salt and pepper and set aside.

In a large, heavy-bottomed saucepan, melt remaining olive oil and butter over medium-low heat. Add onion and cook until softened, about 3 minutes. Add garlic and cook another minute more. Add rice and cook, stirring constantly, until the grains of rice are mostly translucent but with an opaque center, about 3 minutes. Add wine, stirring until the wine is almost completely absorbed. Add a ladle of stock (about ½ to ¾ cup) and stir until almost completely absorbed. Continue adding broth one ladleful at a time and cooking, stirring constantly, until it is absorbed, before adding another ladle of broth. After about 15 minutes, begin tasting the risotto before adding each new ladle of broth. When the rice is nearly done, firm but not crunchy, add another ladleful of broth, along with the morels, favas and pea shoots. Continue stirring, and when the broth has been absorbed, the rice should be *al dente*. Stir in a little more broth along with the Parmesan, then season to taste with salt and pepper. Serve immediately, topped with a few tender pea vine tips.

**Tip**
To shell favas, open the whole bean pod along the seam and pull each bean from the pod. Blanch the beans in salted water for 1 minute, then drain and chill in an ice water bath. Use your fingernails to pinch a bit of skin off one side of the bean. Squeeze the skin at the opposite side to pop the bean out.

# Arugula Pesto

## Makes about 2 cups

One person's "rocket" is another's arugula (it also goes by the names rugula and rucola). Not even heard of in the United States until the 1970s when California Cuisine took hold, arugula now appears regularly on restaurant menus throughout the state. Arugula is in season here from about mid-March to November. In the hot summer months, however, it can get quite bitter. If you are growing it at home, plan for spring and fall harvests for a milder but still peppery flavor.

4 well-packed cups fresh arugula leaves, rinsed and patted dry

4 cloves garlic, peeled

1 cup pine nuts or other nut of your choice

1½ cups freshly grated Parmesan or Pecorino cheese

1½ cups extra virgin olive oil

sea salt and freshly ground pepper to taste

In a blender, pulse arugula and garlic until well crushed. Add nuts, process to crush, then add cheese. You should have a thick paste. Slowly drizzle in olive oil, continuously mixing. Adjust seasoning and serve with pasta (and, as shown in our photo, with grilled shrimp) or vegetables, or add to a soup, etc.

**Variation**
Genoa, Italy, is the birthplace of pesto, where it is traditionally made with basil and pine nuts in a mortar and pestle. A blender or food processor also works just fine—the method is the same. For variety, try other herbs, such as cilantro or even cooked artichokes, or nuts and seeds, such as walnuts and sunflower kernels.

# Braised Swiss Chard

## Serves 4

With its bright red stalks and dark green leaves, this cool-climate lover is an ideal Washington vegetable because it can withstand frost, and when planted in early spring, it is usually ready to eat within four to six weeks. Chard also rivals spinach as a great leafy green because, unlike spinach, it contains no oxalic acid, so the minerals it contains are more readily digestible. Chard is a kind of beet grown for its leaves rather than its roots. It packs a huge amount of vitamin A and is naturally high in sodium—one cup contains 313 mg. It is the perfect spring vegetable because the tips are very tender and it offers a much different taste at this time of the year than in the fall, when it is typically consumed. Try also using chard raw in a salad.

**2 small red onions, chopped**

**1 Tbsp butter**

**2 lbs chard leaves, stems removed**

**¼ cup white wine**

**sea salt and freshly ground pepper to taste**

Sauté the onions in butter over medium heat in a large pan until they are nearly softened and lightly browned, about 8 to 10 minutes. Meanwhile, clean chard leaves (see below) and slice into ribbons.

Add the chard leaves and wine. Cook rapidly, stirring frequently, until the chard is wilted and the liquid has evaporated, about 5 minutes.

Season with salt and pepper, and serve as a side dish. Grilled beef kebabs, as shown in our photo, are a nice complement to braised chard.

### Tip
To clean chard, simply swish in cool water and pat dry. The stems and leaves are both edible, but should be cooked separately because the stems take longer to cook.

Chard can be used instead of spinach or kale in your favorite recipes.

# Potato Frittata

## Serves 4

When people think of comfort food, potatoes are often the first ingredient to come to mind. Luckily, they are easy to find and come in ever-growing variations (25 different varieties were spotted at a local farmers' market recently). Eastern Washington state produces the highest yield per acre of potatoes in the world. It is thought that this incredible potato output is the result of a combination of factors: rich volcanic soil, readily available irrigation, a long growing season and overall climatic conditions. Derived from the Italian word *fritto* ("fried"), a frittata is an open-faced omelette made with cheese and other ingredients mixed into the eggs. It is a classic Roman dish traditionally served on Easter Day. Incorporating potatoes into this breakfast dish makes it an especially satisfying and comforting one-dish meal.

**2 Tbsp butter**

**3 onions, sliced**

**2 medium Yukon Gold or Yellow Finn potatoes, peeled, cooked and sliced**

**8 eggs**

**¾ cup half and half cream (18 percent) or milk**

**sea salt and freshly ground pepper**

**½ cup grated aged Cheddar cheese**

**1 Tbsp chopped fresh thyme**

Preheat broiler to 500° F. Melt butter in a 9-inch nonstick, ovenproof pan over low heat. Add onions and sauté, stirring occasionally, for 10 to 15 minutes until onions are golden brown. Add potato slices and cook until starting to brown, about 5 minutes. Whisk eggs, cream or milk, salt and pepper in a bowl. Pour egg mixture over onions in frying pan and sprinkle with cheese and thyme. Cook frittata for 5 to 6 minutes or until it is almost set. To finish cooking, place frittata under broiler for 1 minute. Cut into wedges and serve along with your breakfast favorites.

*Potatoes have the unique historical distinction of being once thought of as both an aphrodisiac and as a cause of leprosy.*

# Asparagus Omelette

**Serves 1**

A sure sign of spring is the arrival of local asparagus on the shelves at our many green grocers. This unique vegetable takes more than three years from its initial planting to actually start producing the tender shoots that are suitable for harvest. Trust us when we tell you that locally grown asparagus is worth the wait all year. Asparagus is grown primarily in the Columbia Basin, the Yakima Valley and the Walla Walla area. Close to 53 million pounds of asparagus are produced each year, bringing upwards of $28 million to our state's economy.

3 eggs, separated

2 Tbsp cream
(10 to 18 percent)

1 Tbsp unsalted butter

pinch each of sea salt and
freshly ground pepper

6 thin asparagus stalks, or
3 thick, lightly steamed

2 Tbsp goat cheese

1 Tbsp chopped fresh
chives

In a medium bowl, blend egg yolks and cream with a fork. In another bowl, beat the whites until soft peaks form. Gently fold the whites into the yolks. In a nonstick 10-inch pan, melt butter over medium-high heat. Pour in eggs, swirling around pan to distribute evenly. Season with salt and pepper. Using a spatula, push the egg mixture gently around to allow the uncooked egg to flow underneath, running the spatula around the sides of the omelette to loosen. When the eggs are almost set, about 40 seconds, lay the asparagus and cheese in the middle of the omelette. Fold ⅓ of the omelette over the filling, then lift the pan and slide the opposite third onto a plate and fold the omelette onto itself, forming a neat tri-fold package. Sprinkle with chives and serve immediately.

Tip
When buying asparagus, choose firm, bright green stalks for the best flavor.

# Port Madison Goat Yogurt and Honey Semifreddo

## Serves 4 to 6

When most of the rest of us are sleeping, Beverly and Steve Phillips are up milking their 200 Bainbridge Island-raised goats to provide Washingtonians with some of the freshest goat milk, cheese and yogurt to be found anywhere. In the business since 1988, they produce a tangy and light goat milk yogurt that is delicious on its own or semi-frozen and sweetened with honey from any of a dozen or more honey producers found in Washington. Making semifreddo is easier than making ice cream, and using goat's milk yogurt will give this dessert a unique twist.

**2¼ cups heavy cream (32 percent)**

**5 egg yolks**

**½ cup honey**

**½ cup unflavored yogurt**

In a mixer, whisk cream to stiff peaks. Transfer the whipped cream into another bowl and set aside. Clean and dry the mixing bowl and whisk yolks with honey until pale yellow and thickened. Fold in yogurt. Then fold in whipped cream.

Line 4 to 6 small molds with plastic wrap. Place filling into the mold. Cover and freeze for 24 hours. Remove semifreddo from the freezer just before serving. Top with your favorite berries.

*Semifreddo is Italian for "half-cold" and describes the half-frozen or chilled nature of this delicious confection.*

**Tip**
You can use almost any small dish
as a mold for semifreddo, as long
as it has straight or flared sides
and it is freezer-safe.

# Ruth's Unbaked Strawberry Cheesecake

**Serves 8**

The first strawberries of the season signify the start of summer. There are two main types of strawberries: June-bearing, which provide extremely high-quality berries until July, and the lesser quality everbearing type, which extend the season into September. Washington is the fifth-largest strawberry grower in the United States. On Bainbridge Island in Puget Sound, Japanese-American farmers, as well as the Filipino community, raised the majority of the strawberries, and their farms were known as the benchmark of the industry in their time. The Vashon Strawberry Festival is held on Vashon Island every July, and people from all over come to celebrate these little red chunks of summer. For the do-it-yourselfer, strawberries are easy to grow in a container garden on your deck or balcony. This recipe is an unbaked cheesecake, which we find creamier and not as heavy as baked cheesecakes, and it's more suited to the juicy strawberries.

### Crust
**2 cups graham wafer crumbs**

**½ cup + 1 Tbsp unsalted butter, melted**

**finely chopped zest from 1 lemon**

### Filling
**3 x 8 oz packages of cream cheese, at room temperature**

**½ to 1 cup icing sugar, sifted**

**generous squeeze of fresh lemon juice**

**⅓ cup whipping cream (32 percent)**

### Topping
**1 x 8 oz jar of apple jelly**

**1 lb whole strawberries, washed and stemmed**

Preheat oven to 350° F. Crush graham wafers with a rolling pin or pulse in a food processor to make crumbs. In a mixing bowl, combine the graham wafer crumbs, melted butter and lemon zest. Pat the mixture evenly into a 10-inch pie plate. Bake in the oven for 10 minutes. Cool to room temperature. Cover and chill in the refrigerator until ready to fill. Crust can be made a day in advance.

In a food processor, combine cream cheese, icing sugar and lemon juice. Mix until smooth and creamy. Transfer into a large mixing bowl.

In a small bowl, beat the whipping cream until light and fluffy, and fold into the cream cheese mixture. Gently fill the chilled graham crust with the creamy filling and chill for at least 3 hours before serving.

To prepare the topping, gently heat the apple jelly until just warm in a small saucepan. In a medium bowl, pour the warm jelly over the strawberries and mix lightly. Arrange the glazed strawberries on top of the cheesecake.

**Tip**
You can use the bottom of a small glass to help press the graham wafer crumbs evenly on the pie plate.

# Rhubarb Pie with a Meringue Crust

### Serves 6

For early North American pioneers, the robust and hardy rhubarb plant supplied essential vitamins and minerals in spring before any berries ripened. Indigenous to Asia, rhubarb was first brought to Europe for its medicinal qualities. Officially recognized in Europe as a food, rhubarb was known as "pie plant" because it was most often presented as a pie filling and in other desserts. Washington is the largest producer of rhubarb in the nation. Most of the rhubarb is grown around the town of Sumner where the moderate climate and fertile soil make rhubarb grow like a weed. This recipe offers a nice balance between the tart rhubarb and the sweet meringue topping. And remember, don't eat the plant's leaves—they're poisonous.

**1 cup sugar**

**3 Tbsp flour**

**1 tsp cinnamon**

**2 lbs rhubarb, frozen or fresh**

**1 x 9-inch pie crust, prebaked (or see p. 89 for Great Pie Crust)**

Mix together sugar, flour and cinnamon in a large bowl. Slice rhubarb into 1-inch pieces, add to the flour-sugar mixture and mix until well coated.

In a saucepan over medium heat, cook rhubarb until it is soft and thickened, about 10 minutes. Let cool for at least 30 minutes.

### Meringue

**⅓ cup sugar**

**1 Tbsp cornstarch**

**5 egg whites**

**½ tsp cream of tartar**

For the meringue, mix sugar and corn-starch in a small bowl. In another bowl, with an electric mixer, beat egg whites until foamy. Add cream of tartar and beat in sugar-cornstarch mixture, 1 Tbsp at a time, until egg whites are stiff and glossy.

Pour the cooled rhubarb filling into prepared pie crust and spoon meringue gently on top.

Preheat the oven to 350° F. Bake the meringue-topped pie for 10 to 12 minutes, until the meringue is slightly golden.

*A member of the buckwheat family, rhubarb is closely related to sorrel. Although rhubarb is technically a vegetable, the stems are used as a fruit in most recipes.*

# Fresh Pea and Mint Pasta Salad

## Serves 4 to 6

Fresh peas are a hallmark of early summer in western Washington and are a favorite crop among backyard gardeners and commercial growers alike. On the home front, fresh green peas that are shelled at the sink are more likely to be eaten on the spot than make it to the table! A cool-climate crop, peas come into season in June and are available fresh at local farmers' markets, U-pick farms, produce merchants and many grocery stores. Peas can also be grown successfully in the fall, as the cooler weather in September and October enables commercial growers and backyard gardeners another opportunity to coax all that sweetness out of such a little package. Western Washington (and B.C.) produce the highest quality and highest yielding peas in all of North America.

**1 x 12 oz package of pasta, cooked and cooled (see Tip)**

**1 cup halved cherry tomatoes**

**½ small red onion, halved and very thinly sliced**

**2 cups fresh peas**

**2 Tbsp finely chopped fresh mint**

**1 Tbsp finely chopped fresh oregano**

**1 cup chopped roasted chicken (optional)**

In a large bowl, gently toss the pasta, tomatoes, onion, peas, mint, oregano and chicken, if using.

In a small bowl, whisk the dressing ingredients together, pour over the salad and toss again. Serve immediately, or store, covered, in the refrigerator until ready to serve as a side dish.

**Tip**
Pastas such as gemelli, fusilli, rotini or radiatore are perfect for pasta salads because their texture holds the dressing nicely.

**Dressing**

2 Tbsp white wine vinegar

¼ cup olive oil

½ tsp Dijon mustard

3 Tbsp mayonnaise (see p. 7)

sea salt and freshly ground
pepper to taste

# Prawn and Melon Salad

## Serves 4

Eating sustainably harvested seafood has become an important goal so that we can preserve our ocean's bounty. Luckily, there are many sustainable choices in seafood. For this light and refreshing summertime salad, look for local wild-caught pink shrimp, spot prawns or the harder-to-find but delicious coonstripe and sidestripe shrimp.

### Sauce

½ **honeydew melon, peeled and seeded**

¼ **cup honey**

**juice from 2 limes, divided**

**2 tsp sugar**

**coarse sea salt and cayenne pepper to taste**

### Salad

**juice from 2 lemons**

**zest and juice from 2 limes**

**2 Tbsp grape seed oil**

**splash of sesame oil**

**1 lb cooked prawns, peeled, deveined and cut in half or into bite-sized pieces**

½ **honeydew melon, cut into bite-sized pieces**

**1 cup bite-sized watermelon pieces**

⅓ **cup finely chopped mint**

**1 Tbsp black sesame seeds, toasted (see Tip, p. 134)**

**pinch of sugar**

**coarse sea salt and cayenne pepper to taste**

**1 avocado, peeled, seeded and cut in medium dice**

**mint sprigs for garnish**

For the sauce, purée the honeydew melon in a blender. Strain purée through a fine sieve and discard the pulp. Heat the honeydew juice in a small saucepan over medium heat. Add the honey and half the lime juice and reduce until syrupy, about 10 minutes. Stir in the sugar until dissolved. Cool the syrup in its pot over an ice water bath. When chilled, season to taste with salt, cayenne and remaining lime juice. Keep refrigerated until ready to use.

For the salad, combine lemon and lime juices, lime zest and grape seed and sesame oils in a medium-sized bowl; mix well. Add prawns, chopped honeydew and watermelon, mint and sesame seeds; toss gently. Season to taste with sugar, salt and cayenne.

To serve, place ¼ of the avocado in the center of each plate. Top the avocado with the prawn and melon mixture. Spoon the sauce onto the plate around the salad and garnish with a sprig of mint.

Gone are the days of watermelon seed-spitting contests. Seedless watermelons are widely available from local farms. Galia and Charentais melons are worth picking up at your nearest farmers' market as well.

# Tomato Salad with Bocconcini Tempura

**Serves 4**

It is hard to believe that at one time tomatoes were believed to be poisonous and therefore avoided entirely. As members of the nightshade family, tomatoes do contain a small amount of toxic glycoalkaloids (many plants have natural toxins in order to ward off pests). Toxins, however, don't seem to stop the tomato's prime predator—humans—as we continue to grow them widely in our American kitchen gardens. These days, growing organic and heirloom tomatoes is quite popular (a few examples of which are brandywine, green zebra and the mortgage lifter—a tomato so grand that, as the story goes, it helped M.C. Byles pay his mortgage because he was able to sell his plants for a dollar each in the 1940s). Early ripening varieties are the best to grow west of the mountains, as western Washingtonians just don't get enough sustained heat for most tomato varieties. An easy-to-grow and fast-ripening cherry tomato is the very sweet Sun Gold.

**peanut oil for deep frying (see Tip)**

**1 lb assorted heirloom tomatoes, sliced into thick rounds**

**handful of fresh basil**

**1 x 17 oz container of mini bocconcini, drained and patted very dry**

**1 recipe tempura batter (see p. 173)**

**extra virgin olive oil or cold-pressed canola oil**

**juice from 1 lemon**

**sea salt and freshly ground pepper**

Heat peanut oil in pot or deep fryer to 375° F. Arrange sliced tomato and basil onto individual plates. Dip bocconcini into tempura batter and fry until golden. Serve tempura bocconcini together with tomato slices, drizzle with oil and lemon juice. Season with salt and pepper.

**Tip**
For deep-frying, peanut oil should be 2 to 3 inches deep in the pot, or use a deep fryer according to the manufacturer's directions.

*Bocconcini, meaning "small mouthfuls," are a form of semi-ripe mozzarella cheese that come in small, soft, white balls. Watch for ciliegine, "small cherries," which are even smaller portions of the same delicious cheese. A truly fresh mozzarella is a flavor and texture experience like no other. Look for mozzarellas made by Golden Glen Creamery and River Valley Ranch right here in Washington.*

# Banh Xeo

**Serves 4**

Seattle saw a large influx of Vietnamese immigrants arrive in the 1970s. Vietnamese restaurants now thrive here, and most Seattleites can easily name their favorite place for *pho*, and often a different favorite place for *banh mi*, the delicious and inexpensive sandwiches on crusty baguettes. People in the know often have another favorite hole-in-the-wall place where they go to get *banh xeo* (pronounced "bahn sow"). You will be amazed that this dish is egg-free—to all eyes it appears that it is an omelette. This easy-to-make dish gets its yellow hue from turmeric and its delicious flavor from the coconut milk in the batter and the savory-sour-spicy combination of the shrimp and pork filling dipped in *nuoc cham*, the salsa of Vietnam.

**Sauce (*Nuoc Cham*)**
**juice from 2 limes**
**⅓ cup water**
**2 Tbsp sugar**
**3 Thai chilies, minced**
**1 clove garlic, minced**
**1 Tbsp fish sauce**
**1 Tbsp shredded carrot (optional)**

**Crepes**
**2 cups rice flour**
**1 tsp kosher salt**
**1 tsp sugar**
**1 tsp turmeric**
**½ tsp curry powder, Vietnamese or Indian Madras-style**
**4 scallions, sliced, white and green parts**
**½ cup coconut milk**
**2 cups water**
**peanut oil, as needed for cooking crepes**

For the sauce, whisk everything together in a bowl and set aside. For the filling, in a large sauté pan, heat oil over medium-high. Add onion, mushrooms and salt, and sauté until tender, about 10 minutes. Add a splash of water if mixture starts to stick to pan. Add pork and cook for 2 to 3 minutes. Add shrimp and cook until the shrimp are cooked through, 2 more minutes. Add bean sprouts and cook 1 more minute. Taste and adjust seasonings if necessary. Set filling aside and keep warm.

For the crepes, whisk batter ingredients together in a bowl and set aside. Heat a medium-sized nonstick sauté pan over medium-high. Add a film of oil. Wait 30 seconds to heat the oil and then ladle out crepe batter. If it has thickened while you were cooking the filling, thin it out with a few tablespoons of water—it should be the consistency of thin pancake batter. You want a thin layer of batter over the bottom of the pan. Do not disturb the crepe. Let it cook about 5 minutes on one side. Check it carefully by lifting up one edge with a spatula. It should be crisp, lacy and brown. At that point, carefully flip the crepe over onto the other side (using two spatulas might be helpful here). Cook the other side of the crepe in the same manner until brown and crisp. Layer ¼ of the filling over one side of the crepe (like an omelette) and flip half of the crepe over on itself. It may crack, but that's fine.

Serve with the fixings. *Banh xeo* is best eaten by putting a slice of the crepe inside of a piece of leaf lettuce with some herbs and cucumber then dipping it in the *nuoc cham*.

### Filling
1 Tbsp peanut oil

½ medium yellow onion, sliced

¼ lb cremini, shiitake or button mushrooms (or wild, if in season), sliced

¼ tsp salt

¼ lb lean pork (such as boneless top loin chops), sliced thin

½ lb medium shrimp, peeled and deveined

4 cups bean sprouts

### Fixings
1 head of green leaf lettuce, washed and pulled into leaves

½ bunch of cilantro leaves

½ bunch of basil leaves

⅓ cucumber, sliced

# Honey-drizzled Figs with Pecan-crusted Goat Cheese

### Serves 6

The tag team of bees and beekeepers produce myriad honeys on both sides of the Cascade Mountains. On the west side, the bees feed on clovers, blackberries, lavender and wildflowers. East of the mountains, they favor fireweed, black locusts and tree fruit. It's easiest to find local honey at your nearest farmers' market. If you happen to be in Seattle, don't miss a tour of Washington Park Arboretum—a special bonus there is a taste of the Puget Sound Beekeepers Association honey from hives the members keep in the park.

**1 x 8 oz goat cheese log**

**1 cup toasted, chopped pecans, plus halves for garnish (see Tip, p. 134)**

**1 lb baby mixed lettuce**

**⅓ cup extra virgin olive oil**

**sea salt and freshly ground pepper**

**12 fresh figs, any variety**

**½ cup clover honey**

Roll goat cheese log in nuts, and wrap in cellophane. Refrigerate at least ½ hour and up to 6 hours.

Arrange lettuce onto 6 plates and sprinkle lightly with olive oil. Season with salt and pepper. Cut figs into halves and arrange atop greens.

Slice cheese into 6 equal-sized rounds and place next to figs. Drizzle with honey, season lightly again with salt and pepper and serve.

*For every pound of honey produced, bees fly over 31,000 miles, which is more than once around the Earth.*

# Gazpacho with Fresh Tomato Water

### Serves 8

Gazpacho is a cold soup with origins in Spain. It is typically served during the warm summer months using a combination of ingredients, including stale bread, garlic, olive oil, salt and vinegar. It wasn't until the early 16th century that the tomato and bell pepper were introduced to the ingredient list. During August and September, heirloom tomatoes come into season from specialty growers such as Billy's Gardens in Tonasket. These tomatoes are as sweet as candy, and they create a soup that is beyond compare, as if the flavor of the summer sun were caught in your bowl. Be sure to also check out TomatoFare, held this past year at the Center for American Food & Wine at SageCliffe in Grant County, where you can sample over 70 different organic heirloom tomatoes.

**8 ripe tomatoes, peeled, seeded and finely chopped**

**1 small red onion, finely chopped**

**1 medium English cucumber, peeled, seeded and finely chopped**

**1 red pepper, finely chopped**

**¼ cup chopped fresh parsley**

**¼ cup chopped fresh chives**

**1 clove garlic, minced**

**¼ cup red wine vinegar**

**¼ cup olive oil**

**juice from ½ or 1 lemon**

**2 tsp sugar**

**sea salt and freshly ground pepper to taste**

**6 or more drops of Tabasco sauce**

**4 cups Tomato Water (see opposite)**

Combine all ingredients. Cover tightly and refrigerate overnight for the best flavor. Serve gazpacho cold with some crusty fresh ciabatta bread.

**Tomato Water**
Roughly chop 2 lbs ripe tomatoes
and mix with 1 Tbsp salt. Line a fine
sieve with dampened cheesecloth
and set over a large bowl. Pour the
tomatoes into the sieve, making sure
that the cheesecloth is tied securely,
and let the tomatoes sit for at least
12 hours for all the tomato water to
drain into the bowl.

# Sweet Corn Bisque

### Serves 6

Summer days are long and hot in August, and for many families, they are the perfect time to hit the road and head to the Gypsy Rows Company farm in Silvana. Summer is also corn season, and people return year after year to their favorite road-side stands with claims that they have found the sweetest corn in the state. For those who are stuck in the city, fresh-picked corn is trucked in, usually from east of the Cascades, and appears at farmers' markets, where people will line up for a taste of summer. Although nothing is as good as corn eaten off the cob, this bisque is a refined way to enjoy the sweetness of the summer sun.

**8 cups corn kernels, fresh from the cob or frozen; reserve 2 cups for garnish**

**¼ cup butter, plus 1 Tbsp**

**sea salt and freshly ground pepper to taste**

**2 cups chopped yellow onion**

**1 clove garlic, minced**

**3 stalks celery, diced**

**2 medium carrots, diced**

**2 sprigs fresh thyme, minced**

**6 cups chicken or vegetable stock**

**1 cup heavy cream (32 percent)**

**tarragon sprigs and thinly sliced red pepper for garnish**

**Tabasco sauce to taste**

In a pot, sauté reserved corn in 1 Tbsp of butter until cooked, about 5 minutes. Season with salt and pepper and set aside. In same pot, sauté onions in ¼ cup of butter until translucent. Add garlic, celery and carrots, and sauté for 5 minutes. Add remaining corn and thyme, cover with stock and simmer for 20 minutes. Purée in batches in blender to make a smooth soup, and return to heat. Stir in cream, and season with salt, pepper and Tabasco. Garnish each bowl with reserved corn, tarragon and red pepper. Serve hot with Corn Bread (see opposite).

### Corn Bread

Preheat oven to 400° F and butter two 1-lb loaf pans. Sift together flour, baking powder and salt. Stir in cornmeal. In a separate bowl, cream butter and sugar together, then beat in eggs, one at a time. Stir in buttermilk, then lightly fold wet and dry mixtures together, being sure not to over mix. Spoon into loaf pans and bake for 30 to 35 minutes or until tester comes out clean.

**2 cups flour**

**1 Tbsp baking powder**

**1 tsp sea salt**

**2 cups cornmeal**

**1¼ cups butter**

**⅓ cup sugar**

**3 eggs**

**2 cups buttermilk**

### Tip

To check corn for ripeness, carefully pull the husk open a little bit. Look at the top third to get a sense of the whole cob: if the kernels are tinted red or dented, the corn is overripe; pointed kernels and a dull white color indicate the corn is under ripe. Ideally, you're looking for plump and shiny kernels. A fingernail stabbed into a kernel should reveal milky sap if ripe, doughy sap if overripe. Lean on the side of under ripeness if need be.

# Dungeness Crab and Coconut Soup

### Serves 4 to 6

Come late summer, the days are still warm but evening comes sooner and a chill starts to be felt at night. Washingtonians reluctantly prepare for fall, but the fruits of summer are just as bountiful as ever. Local Dungeness crab, available year-round, is best through August. The price of corn beckons buyers with screaming deals of six ears for a dollar. Bulbous pale green fennel bulbs, sometimes with their feathery tops, sometimes without, are displayed next to the season's last bunches of basil. This soup celebrates the end of summer with light, yet warming flavors.

**2 Tbsp olive oil**

**2 cups thinly sliced yellow onion**

**1 tsp toasted fennel seeds**

**1 fresh red chili, seeded and cut into slivers**

**2 cups fresh corn kernels cut from the cob, with cobs reserved (about 3 to 4 ears)**

**4 cups chicken stock**

**½ Tbsp cornstarch**

**2½ cups coconut milk**

**juice and zest from 1 lime**

**1 lb Dungeness crabmeat, cleaned (see Tip, p. 66)**

**1 cup thinly sliced fresh fennel bulb**

**coarse sea salt and freshly ground pepper to taste**

**¼ cup chopped cilantro leaves**

**¼ cup chopped fresh basil**

In a large saucepan, heat chicken stock to a low simmer. Add corn cobs, cover and simmer for 10 to 15 minutes.

Meanwhile, in a second large saucepan, heat olive oil over medium. Add onions, fennel seeds and chilies. Sauté until softened, about 5 minutes.

Strain chicken stock and add to vegetable mixture; discard cobs. Dissolve the cornstarch in the coconut milk and add to broth along with the lime zest. Bring to a simmer and cook for 5 minutes. Add corn kernels, crab and fennel, and cook until warmed through, about 3 to 5 minutes. Add lime juice. Taste and adjust seasoning. Stir in the cilantro and basil just before serving. Serve hot in bowls.

# Cedar-planked Sockeye Salmon with Orange-Pistachio Crust

### Serves 4 to 6

Abundant year-round and easily harvested along spawning routes, salmon are traditionally key resources for West Coast Native Americans. Equally abundant and important were the cedar trees on the coast. It made sense for the Native American people to cook their freshly caught salmon on easily split cedar planks. They filleted the salmon and cooked it skin-side down, secured to the plank with saplings. The plank was then propped at an angle above the fire, thus perfuming the meat with a delicate, smoky cedar flavor. Home cooks can still use this traditional preparation today. Just remember, always use wild salmon and be sure to soak the cedar plank for at least two hours before cooking.

**1 cup chopped unsalted, shelled pistachios**

**⅔ cup panko (see p. 69)**

**2 Tbsp olive oil**

**1 Tbsp chopped fresh dill**

**2 tsp Dijon mustard**

**zest from 1 orange**

**¼ cup orange juice**

**4 to 6 skin-on sockeye salmon fillets, about 8 oz each**

**2 cedar planks (see Tip)**

**sea salt and freshly ground pepper to taste**

Preheat grill to medium-high. Mix pistachios and panko together—it works especially well to pulse them together in a food processor. Place on a plate and set aside.

Mix oil, dill, mustard, zest and orange juice to form a paste. Spread paste evenly on flesh side of each salmon fillet, then dip in pistachio and panko mixture. As they are crusted, lay the fillets skin-side down on prepared planks. Season crust with sea salt and freshly ground pepper. Place planks on grill, close lid and cook 12 to 15 minutes.

*If not available at your supermarket, get shelled, unsalted pistachios at a Mediterranean or Middle Eastern food store.*

**Tip**
Purchase untreated cedar planks, 1 inch thick, 8 inches wide and 12 inches long, from your local lumberyard or gourmet shop or via the Internet. The planks must be soaked in water for a minimum of 2 hours, but 4 to 6 hours is best. Drain and pat dry; brush with oil before using. Planks can often be cleaned and reused several times.

# Grilled Rainbow Trout with Wild Huckleberry-Lavender Reduction

### Serves 6

The Cascade huckleberry is one of several varieties found in Washington's higher elevations. It is a favorite of hikers, so map your late August and early September Cascade or Olympic Mountains excursions on trails that climb to 2000 feet or higher to get in on the action. Huckleberries tend to grow along lakesides and in open meadows. Slopes with good, sunny, southern exposures are the ideal growing conditions. When you get the berries home, remove all stems and under ripe or damaged berries. Freeze them on a cookie sheet and then transfer to resealable freezer bags, making sure to get all the air out of the bag. When you are ready to use the berries, thaw them the night before in the refrigerator or run cold water over them in the sink for a quick thaw.

### Sauce
1 cup champagne vinegar
1 cup wild huckleberries
¾ cup granulated sugar
½ tsp dried lavender
¼ tsp sea salt

### Fish
6 rainbow trout fillets, 6 to 8 oz each
sea salt and freshly ground pepper

Combine all the ingredients for the sauce in a small saucepan. Bring to a low simmer and cook until the mixture is reduced by about half and coats the back of a spoon. Use a wooden spoon to press the sauce through a fine-meshed sieve.

Clean grill thoroughly with a wire brush. Use a rag to rub a little vegetable oil on the grill, then preheat to medium-high.

While the sauce is reducing, cook the fish. Season the fillets with salt and pepper. Place on the grill skin-side up. Cook until the thinnest edge becomes opaque, about 3 to 5 minutes, depending on thickness. Slip a long spatula under the fillet from

*Steamed green beans lightly dressed with lemon oil (see opposite) make the perfect match for this dish—once you try this oil, you'll find a multitude of ways to use it up.*

the side, lifting the entire fillet at once, to flip. If the fillet sticks at all, leave it for another 30 seconds before trying again. Cook on the second side only to brown the outside, about 2 minutes more.

To serve, place each fillet on a plate and spoon sauce around fillets and over one half.

### Lemon Oil

Place oil in a small saucepan over medium-low heat. When the oil is warm, add the zest. Simmer about 5 minutes, then turn off heat and let stand, uncovered, about 30 minutes before removing zest. Store the lemon oil in the fridge for up to 2 weeks.

**Lemon Oil**
½ cup grape seed oil

zest from 2 lemons, cut off in strips with a peeler rather than zested (if you get any of the pith, slice it off with a small, sharp knife)

# Dungeness Crab Cakes
## Serves 6

Want to start a fight in a bar in Washington state? Simply say that Maryland's blue crab is far superior to our native Dungeness. Them's fightin' words in these parts! Dungeness crab season usually begins in December and runs most of the year, skipping a few months in the fall when the crabs molt. Named after a small fishing village on the Strait of Juan de Fuca, Dungeness crab meat is sweet, succulent and plentiful. Why spend all that time picking the meat out of an undersized blue crab when one large Dungeness will happily satisfy the biggest of appetites? Dungeness crab meat is almost perfect in its naked form—these crab cakes have just a few ingredients because we don't want to mask the flavor of this West Coast treasure.

**1½ lbs Dungeness crabmeat, cleaned (see Tip, below)**

**1 yellow onion, diced**

**1 red bell pepper, diced**

**1 stalk celery, diced**

**2 Tbsp chopped fresh tarragon**

**zest from 1 lemon**

**pinch of cayenne pepper**

**1 Tbsp Worcestershire sauce**

**2 tsp Dijon mustard**

**sea salt and freshly ground pepper to taste**

**2 eggs, lightly beaten**

**seasoned fine bread-crumbs, enough to bind cakes, plus about 3 cups for dredging**

**flour, seasoned with salt and pepper**

**1 whole egg, beaten, for eggwash**

Sauté onion, bell pepper and celery until onion is translucent. Add tarragon, lemon zest, cayenne and Worcestershire sauce to vegetable mixture and let cool to room temperature.

Preheat oven to 375° F. Mix crabmeat, vegetable mixture, Dijon mustard, salt, pepper and 2 beaten eggs with enough breadcrumbs to hold cakes together. Form into ⅓-cup cakes. Dredge cakes in seasoned flour, then in eggwash and finally in seasoned breadcrumbs.

Heat pan to medium and pan-fry cakes until golden. Transfer to a baking sheet and finish cooking in oven, about 7 to 10 minutes. Serve hot with Chipotle Remoulade (see opposite).

**Tip**
To clean crabmeat, remove all cartilage and shells.

**Chipotle Remoulade**
Mix all ingredients together and refrigerate at least 4 hours or up to 1 week.

**Tip**
For best flavor, the Chipotle Remoulade must be made at least 4 hours before serving.

*Chipotles are delicious and very spicy smoked jalapeño peppers, often found canned in adobe sauce. Try the Mexican section at the super-market, or find a Mexican specialty grocer.*

1½ cups mayonnaise
(see p. 7)

1 Tbsp grainy mustard

about 1 tsp minced chipotle peppers in adobo sauce,
or to taste

½ cup finely diced green onions

1 Tbsp chopped capers

1 tsp minced garlic

¼ cup finely chopped parsley

juice of ¼ lemon

sea salt and freshly ground pepper to taste

# Panko and Coconut Spot Prawns

**Serves 6**

Spot prawns are named for the distinctive white spots that adorn their shells. Highly regarded for their size and flavor, spot prawns are the largest of the seven shrimp species caught commercially in the Pacific Northwest's coastal waters; females are known to grow to nine inches in length or more. Spot prawns are available frozen year-round, but look for them fresh from Washington waters during the summer. Remarkably succulent and sweet, spot prawns are caught with pots, widely agreed to be the most sustainable fishing method. Pots have few environmental impacts and hardly any "bycatch" (the name for other species caught and often killed in the process).

1 cup flour

sea salt and freshly ground pepper

3 eggs, beaten

1 cup panko (see opposite)

½ cup shredded unsweetened coconut

24 spot prawns, shelled, deveined, tail on

4 cups peanut oil, for frying

½ cup Thai chili dipping sauce

Place flour in a bowl or shallow baking dish, and season with salt and pepper. Beat eggs in a separate bowl. Combine panko and coconut in another shallow dish. Dredge prawns first in flour, then in beaten eggs and finally coat in panko mixture. Carefully lay prawns out in a single layer on a baking sheet.

Pour oil into a heavy-bottomed skillet and heat to 360° F; if you do not have a thermometer, test oil with a cube of bread—it should turn golden in under 2 minutes. Cook prawns in small batches until golden, about 2 minutes, then transfer to a plate lined with a paper towel. Serve hot with dipping sauce.

**Tip**

Whenever possible, buy your prawns with heads on. Keeping them whole is worth the extra work and ensures the flavorful juices are retained in the flesh. Thaw frozen prawns in the refrigerator overnight and use immediately.

*Panko is a Japanese-style breadcrumb that is now popular enough to be widely available in most grocery stores (or visit an Asian specialty grocer). It is an ultra-white, extra-coarse breadcrumb that stays particularly crispy when fried.*

# Pacific Scallops with Bacon and Vanilla

**Serves 4**

Wild weathervane scallops are always a treat, but when paired with bacon and a hint of vanilla, they are transcendent. Widely known as the largest scallop you can get, weathervanes are from the clean, cold waters of southeast Alaska. The scallop fishery is sustainably managed, offering just 10 boats the rights to fish for scallops. The scallops are harvested by lowering large dredges into the mostly sandy sea floor in strictly defined areas. The boats process and freeze the scallops onboard individually, making it very easy to thaw exactly what you need. Try the scallops with green alder smoked bacon from Sea Breeze Farm on Vashon Island.

⅔ cup diced bacon

2 Tbsp minced shallots

1 cup dry Washington sparkling wine

½ vanilla bean pod

½ tsp champagne vinegar, plus extra for dressing

1 cup cold unsalted butter, cut into small pieces

sea salt and freshly ground white pepper to taste

12 Pacific scallops

1 bunch of watercress, tough stems removed, cleaned and spun dry

1 Tbsp olive oil, plus extra for dressing

fresh chives for garnish

In a medium saucepan, sauté bacon until crispy. Drain and set aside. Place shallots, sparkling wine, vanilla bean pod and seeds in small saucepan, and bring to a boil. Reduce heat to medium-low and simmer until you have about ¼ cup of liquid remaining. Stir in champagne vinegar and remove vanilla pod. Turn heat down to very low and, little by little, whisk in butter, 1 piece at a time. Continue until all butter pieces have been added and sauce will coat back of a spoon. Stir in bacon, and season sauce with salt and pepper. Keep sauce warm but off direct heat until ready to serve.

Season scallops on all sides with salt and pepper. Place olive oil in a large pan over medium-high heat. When oil is hot, add scallops and sear for 2 to 3 minutes, until nicely caramelized. Turn scallops over and cook for an additional 3 minutes.

For dressing, toss watercress in a bowl with a splash of olive oil and champagne vinegar, and season with salt and pepper. Serve scallops immediately with sauce, watercress and chives.

**Tip**
To get the most flavor out of a vanilla
bean pod, carefully slice it open and
scrape out the tiny seeds; use both
seeds and pod in the recipe.

# Skagit River Ranch Beef Burger

## Serves 4

The hamburger originated in Hamburg, Germany—sort of. There was no bun, no ketchup and no drive-through; it was just a ground-meat patty known as "Hamburg Steak." Over the years, several Americans have claimed credit for inventing the burger as we know it, leading at times to heated controversy. It is generally agreed that the burger first reached national exposure during the St. Louis World's Fair in 1904. Hamburgers form the backbone of the fast-food industry, but that doesn't mean they are inherently unhealthy. Certified organic in 1998 by the Washington State Department of Agriculture, Skagit River Ranch raises 150 Angus cattle on the Skagit River in Sedro-Woolley. Grass-fed beef are high in healthful omega-3 fatty acids and conjugated linoleic acid (CLA), an antioxidant and potentially healthful fat.

$1\frac{1}{2}$ lbs ground beef

1 egg

1 Tbsp grainy Dijon mustard

$\frac{1}{3}$ cup fine breadcrumbs

sea salt and freshly ground pepper

Preheat grill to high. Mix all ingredients together and form into 4 thick patties; thick patties mean juicy burgers.

Grill patties, turning once, for 4 to 6 minutes per side, until internal temperature reaches 160° F. Serve patties on toasted buns with your favorite accompaniments.

### Tip
For a better burger...

- Handling the meat lightly when mixing and shaping will help prevent it from turning into a hockey puck.

- Make sure the grill is hot to seal in the juices and keep the meat from sticking.

- When shaping your patties, sneak a piece of your favorite cheese (e.g., Bleu, Brie or Cheddar) in the center, making sure it is completely surrounded by the meat, for a volcanic cheeseburger.

Here are some food safety tips when handling raw meat.

- *Store it in the refrigerator and use it within 2 days, or freeze it.*
- *Wash your hands and everything the meat contacted with a solution of 1 tsp unscented bleach per quart of water.*
- *Do not place the cooked burgers on the same surface the raw meat was on.*
- *Cook ground meat until it reaches 160° F in temperature. E. coli is of particular concern for children, the elderly or anyone with a compromised immune system.*

# Full Circle Farm Potato Salad

## Serves 4 to 6

Down a long road, past the tractors and the horses, a big red iconic barn comes into view ahead. The Cascade Mountains and the Snoqualmie River provide gorgeous scenery, framing the 120 acres that is Andrew Stout and Wendy Munro's Full Circle Farm. In business for over 10 years, Full Circle grows organic produce for a whopping 500 community-supported agriculture ("CSA") members, as well as area restaurants, farmers' markets, grocery stores and wholesalers. Known not only for their bountiful produce but also for their community activism around sustainable agricultural issues, Full Circle is a pioneer in enriching their land and their community. For this recipe, try to use Full Circle Farm's fingerling potatoes for their rich and buttery texture.

2 lbs potatoes, scrubbed

sea salt

2 carrots, diced

2 celery stalks, diced

1 x 8 oz jar of artichoke hearts, well drained and rinsed, then drained again and cut into eighths

1 green onion, white part only, finely chopped

1 red pepper, diced into small pieces

6 black olives, pitted and cut into slivers

6 baby gherkins, thinly sliced

¼ cup finely chopped parsley

1 Tbsp drained, chopped capers

¼ tsp sea salt

freshly ground black pepper

mayonnaise (see p. 7)

Cook the potatoes in gently boiling salted water, until just tender. Once cooled, peel the potatoes, cut into smallish cubes and set aside in a bowl. Meanwhile, cook the carrots in gently boiling salted water for 5 minutes, then drain and refresh with cold water and dry them on a paper towel. Combine carrots and the rest of the ingredients with the potatoes and mix enough mayonnaise for a nice creamy texture. Taste and adjust seasonings. Serve, or chill until ready to serve.

Structured in myriad ways depending on the farm, community-supported agriculture ("CSA") shares enable "members" or "shareholders" to receive a part of the farm's harvest throughout the growing season. Some are set up so that you receive a box at your door, full of that farm's seasonal produce often with a recipe or two in the box to help you out. Some have a neighborhood pick-up area, and still others pick produce on the farm. CSA subscriptions help farmers pay for their upcoming growing season and are a terrific way to learn about what is in season in your area, all the while eating extremely fresh food and supporting your local farmer.

# Minted Coleslaw

## Serves 8

Often regarded as a health food, cabbage has been cultivated since before recorded history—although at first it was merely a few leaves and no head. Pythagoras recommended cabbage for longevity, and he lived to be over 80. The word coleslaw comes from the medieval Dutch *kool sla*, meaning "cabbage salad." Today, coleslaw graces nearly every picnic and barbecue in the land. Mint elevates this recipe from the mainstream into something memorable. At farmers' markets you can find great big green bunches of mint for $1.50; an incredible bargain considering supermarket mint (when you can find it) is often $3 to $4 for a few wilted stems.

**2 Tbsp grainy Dijon mustard**

**2 Tbsp sour cream**

**1 Tbsp mayonnaise (see p. 7)**

**1 Tbsp olive oil**

**2 Tbsp apple cider vinegar**

**1 head of Savoy cabbage, shredded**

**1 small head of red cabbage, shredded (about 2 cups)**

**1 fennel bulb, shredded**

**1 carrot, grated**

**6 radishes, grated**

**½ cup sliced green onion**

**½ cup thinly sliced fresh mint**

Whisk together first 5 ingredients for dressing. Toss vegetables together in a large bowl and add dressing. Toss well and let marinate at least 30 minutes before serving.

**Tip**
You can easily turn this recipe into an Asian slaw by omitting sour cream, mayonnaise, olive oil and mint and substituting 1 Tbsp toasted sesame oil, 1 Tbsp soy sauce and a handful of toasted sesame seeds. Grilled and sliced turkey or chicken breast also makes a nice addition.

# Summer Squash Ratatouille

## Serves 4 as a main course, 6 as a side dish

This traditional French Provençal stew makes great use of the bounty of summer squash. Adding *herbes de Provence* gives the ratatouille an authentic flavor with hints of lavender reminiscent of the French hillsides. The difference between summer squash and winter squash is in their shelf life and flavor. Winter squash, such as pumpkins, develop hard rinds and can be stored for months, whereas summer squash, such as zucchini, are best eaten before they mature and develop a bitter flavor. In Washington, summer squash is plentiful—many home gardeners grow more than they can ever use, so the next time your neighbor gives you zucchini, try using it for this recipe.

1 medium eggplant (2½ lbs) cut into ½-inch cubes

olive oil for cooking

1 lb assorted summer squash, as much variety as possible, cut into ½-inch slices

2 medium onions, sliced

2 red bell peppers, seeded and cut into ½-inch strips

3 (about 1 lb) ripe but firm tomatoes, seeded and quartered

2 cloves garlic, minced

⅓ cup of a mixture of chopped fresh rosemary, thyme, basil, fennel and marjoram

pinch of dried lavender

sea salt and freshly ground pepper to taste

French bread

Lay the eggplant cubes on paper towels and sprinkle with salt. Let them sit for 15 minutes, then rinse and pat dry.

Have a large bowl ready. Place a splash of olive oil in a large skillet or casserole over medium heat. Add the eggplant chunks and cook until they start to soften, remove from pan and set aside in the bowl to make room for the next vegetable. Add more olive oil, as needed, and continue with the squash, onions and peppers separately.

Return all vegetables to pan; add tomatoes, garlic and herbs. Season with salt

and pepper and stir to mix. Simmer over medium heat until much of the liquid is evaporated, about 10 minutes, then cover. Turn heat to medium-low and cook until the vegetables are tender, about 45 minutes to 1 hour, stirring occasionally to prevent sticking. Serve at room temperature with crusty French bread.

Tip
Squash blossoms are also edible and make a great vessel for stuffing and deep frying. Make sure you choose the male stems (but leave a few for pollination) and leave the fruit-bearing females for an abundant summer supply.

# Grilled Corn with Jalapeño Lime Butter

Many of our region's warmest counties, including Grant County (top sweet corn-producing county in the U.S.A.), produce the country's sweetest corn because of the combination of hot summer days and cooler nights—optimal conditions for increasing the sugar content. This recipe combines one of summer's greatest treasures with a Mexican-inspired butter that will have you heating up the barbecue all summer long.

**ears of corn**

**Jalapeño Lime Butter (see below)**

**lime wedges**

**sea salt to taste**

**Jalapeño Lime Butter**

**1 cup unsalted butter, softened**

**1 jalapeño pepper, seeded and finely chopped**

**zest from 1 lime**

**1 clove garlic, minced**

**1 tsp sea salt**

Preheat the barbecue to medium-high. Peel back the husks, leaving them attached, and remove the silk from the corn. Rewrap the corn, tying with butcher's twine or kitchen string if necessary. Barbecue for about 10 minutes, turning to cook all sides. If husks start to burn, spritz with water.

Serve hot corn with rounds of Jalapeño Lime Butter, lime wedges and sea salt.

### Jalapeño Lime Butter

Mix the ingredients together in a bowl or in a food processor. Wrap in plastic and shape into a cylinder about an inch in diameter, and refrigerate.

*Sweet corn, which is the corn that we eat fresh, is the result of a gene mutation in field corn. This mutation occurred in the 1800s in the United States and prevented sugar in the kernel from being converted to starch.*

# Barbecued Peaches with Camembert

**Serves 6**

"The perfect dessert after a rich and satisfying meal is a perfect piece of fruit, and the most perfect fruit has to be a perfect peach," says Alice Waters, the mother of the seasonal, local food movement. Indeed, it takes a humble chef with deep respect for ingredients to present a perfect peach on a napkin as the final course to an outstanding meal. You know when you have a perfect peach: the fuzzy skin is thin and yields easily as you taste the bright orange, slightly floral flesh. A perfect peach should make you giggle, as rivulets of sweet juice run down your chin with abandon.

**6 peaches, pitted and sliced in half**

**2 Tbsp canola or grape seed oil**

**1 Tbsp honey**

**pinch each of sea salt and freshly ground pepper**

**4 oz Camembert, cut into wedges**

**6 fresh basil leaves**

Preheat barbecue to medium-high. Combine oil, honey, salt and pepper in a bowl. Brush peaches with glaze and grill, flesh-side down, for 3 minutes. Place peaches flesh-side up on a baking sheet and place a basil leaf and a wedge of Camembert on top of each peach. Return the peaches on baking sheet to the barbecue, close the lid and cook until the cheese is melted, about 5 minutes.

*Peaches are the stone fruit from a tree that originated in China, where peaches are an important symbol for a long life and immortality.*

# Plum Clafoutis

## Serves 8

Strolling the market stalls of Pike Place Market when the first hints of autumn are in the air often reveals box after box of plums of every variety: long, slender, tart Italian plums and round Japanese plums in vibrant shades of yellow, orange, crimson and deep purple. Seattleites proudly celebrated Pike Place Market's centennial this year. Holding a sun-kissed Satsuma plum in your hand and looking out over Puget Sound toward the Olympic Mountains gives you the sense that you are not the first person to have this moment on the famous cobblestone streets of the market.

1 cup milk

1 vanilla bean, split

½ cup butter, plus more
for greasing

3 eggs

½ cup white sugar

pinch of salt

1 cup flour, sifted

10 plums, halved and pitted
(or enough to fill the pan)

confectioner's sugar,
for garnish

Pour milk into a small saucepan. Scrape the seeds from the vanilla bean into the milk, then drop the pod in. Bring almost to a boil over medium heat. Stir in ½ cup butter. Once the butter is melted, remove from heat.

In a medium bowl, lightly beat the eggs. Add sugar and salt and beat until the mixture lightens in color. Add flour all at once and beat until well mixed. Remove the vanilla pod from the milk and slowly pour in milk, beating constantly, until batter is smooth and shiny. Set aside to rest for 30 minutes.

Preheat oven to 400° F. Grease the bottom and sides of a 9- to 10-inch round cake pan. Arrange plums skin-side up in the pan. Rewhisk batter if necessary and pour over plums. Bake until batter is golden brown on top and not quite set in the middle (but almost), about 30 to 40 minutes. Let sit for 15 minutes, then turn out onto a plate and sprinkle with confectioner's sugar to serve.

*Keep your eye out for the fruit known as a "pluot," a cross between a plum and an apricot (¾ plum and ¼ apricot), known for its sweetness and juiciness.*

# Lemon Shortbread-topped Blackberry Cobbler

**Serves 4**

Blackberries are an invasive weed in western Washington. But one person's backyard annoyance is another's bounty. A new trend in these parts is to rent a goat to help keep the blackberry bushes in check. A better idea would be to first invite your friends over with buckets to harvest the berries before the goats have their fill. Use your harvest to make this classic blackberry cobbler with a unique lemon shortbread topping. Leftover shortbread dough can be re-rolled and made into cookies. Just bake them afterwards in your 375° F oven for 10 to 15 minutes.

**Shortbread**
½ lb butter
½ cup confectioner's sugar
1 egg, lightly beaten
½ tsp vanilla extract
zest from 1 lemon
1 cup all-purpose flour
1 cup rice flour
½ tsp baking powder
¼ tsp sea salt

In the bowl of a mixer, use the paddle attachment to cream the butter until fluffy. Add the sugar slowly and beat until it is incorporated. Beat in the egg, then add vanilla and lemon zest and mix well.

In a medium bowl, sift together the two flours, the baking powder and the salt. Add half this mixture to the mixer and beat until it is all incorporated. Add the remaining flour mixture and beat until just combined. Form the dough into a disc, wrap with plastic, and chill for about 30 minutes in the fridge.

Preheat oven to 375° F. Butter the bottoms and sides of 4 teacups or 1-cup soufflé dishes.

**Filling**
6 cups fresh blackberries
½ cup granulated sugar
2 Tbsp cornstarch
¾ tsp ground allspice
1 Tbsp butter

Taste the berries to judge how sweet they are. If they are very sweet, you'll want to use less sugar; if they are very tart, you'll want to use more. In a large mixing bowl, blend sugar, cornstarch and allspice. Add the blackberries and toss gently. Distribute the berries evenly among the dishes (they should be heaped in the cups) and dot with butter. Bake until the berry mixture begins to bubble, about 15 minutes. Remove from the oven.

On a lightly floured cutting board, roll out the dough to about $\frac{1}{2}$ inch thick. Use a fifth teacup or a cookie cutter to cut circles to fit the cups. Cut a hole in the middle to let the steam escape. Place the dough over the hot berries in each cup. Return to the oven and cook until the shortbread turns a pale golden color, about 15 to 20 minutes. Remove from the oven and let cool 10 minutes before serving.

**Tip**
The rice flour helps give this shortbread topping its light texture, but if you don't have rice flour, you can substitute 1 cup all-purpose flour, for a total of 2 cups.

# Cherry Pie

**Serves 6 to 8**

There are several iconic foods that speak of this region: salmon, apples and fine wine come immediately to mind. Heading up that list, however, has to be the Washington state cherry. Our state is the largest producer of sweet cherries in the country. Cherries are big business here, with the delicate, sunny yellow and red Rainiers (a cross between, strangely enough, two dark red varieties, the Bing and the Van cherry) fetching $5 to $6 a pound. Deep red Bings are better known, but one of our favorites is the sour pie cherry Montmorency, which gives pies a classic, complex cherry flavor with a healthy dose of tang. Most of our cherries are exported to Japan, Taiwan and Canada, but enough stay around locally for makeshift roadside stands to vie for our attention come cherry season from early June through the end of July.

**6 cups pitted, fresh sour cherries**

**¾ cup sugar**

**juice from 1 lemon**

**2 Tbsp cornstarch**

**Great Pie Crust (see opposite)**

Preheat oven to 400° F. In a medium saucepan, mix cherries and sugar and cook over medium-low heat until most of the juice from the cherries has reduced, about 15 minutes. Stir the lemon juice and cornstarch together in a small bowl and add to the cherries. Cook, stirring until thick, about 7 minutes. Remove from heat and let cool to room temperature.

Pour cherry filling into a prepared pastry crust and bake for 10 minutes. Reduce heat to 375° F and bake for 20 to 30 minutes or until pastry is golden brown. Let it cool before serving.

### Great Pie Crust

Mix flour, salt and sugar in a bowl. Using your cheese grater, grate frozen butter into flour mixture. Toss lightly to distribute butter, and add lemon juice and enough water for dough just to come together. Divide in half, wrap each piece in plastic wrap and flatten into a disc. Chill for at least 30 minutes before using. Makes enough for a double-crusted pie.

2½ cups flour

1 tsp sea salt

1 Tbsp sugar

1 cup unsalted butter, frozen

1 Tbsp lemon juice

about ⅓ cup ice water

### Tip

To make a lattice top, roll out and cut the remaining piece of dough into 1-inch strips. Interlock the strips in a criss-cross weave over the pie filling and press the strips onto the edges of the bottom crust. Brush the pastry lightly with a glaze made with 1 beaten egg and 2 Tbsp milk.

# Raspberry Tart

### Serves 6 to 8

Fragrantly sweet and subtly tart, raspberries are yet another of Washington's top producing crops. Where are all of these rich-red, finger-staining berries coming from? Whatcom County is the nation's top raspberry-producing county. Every year, the town of Lynden (just south of the Canadian border) hosts a Raspberry Festival. Folks run a 5K through fields bursting with the season's crop. Not too far away, the McPhail family farm, in the farming business for three generations, has U-pick raspberries (along with logan-, marion-, black-, goose-, tay-, boysen- and strawberries.)

### Crust

1¼ cups all-purpose flour

¼ cup sugar

½ cup or 1 stick unsalted butter, cold and cut into pieces

2 to 3 Tbsp cold water

### Filling

2 x 8 oz containers of mascarpone, room temperature

½ cup sugar

1 tsp vanilla

3 cups raspberries, picked over

### Glaze

1 x 8 oz jar of apple jelly

For the crust, place flour, sugar and butter in a food processor and blend until mixture resembles coarse meal. Add 2 Tbsp of the water until incorporated. Add enough remaining water, if necessary, until mixture comes together but is still crumbly. Wrap dough in plastic and refrigerate for 1 hour.

Preheat oven to 350° F. Press crust mixture evenly onto bottom and sides of an 11-inch tart pan with removable fluted rim or 6 to 8 individual tart tins. Prick crust with a fork, line it with parchment and weigh it down with pie weights or dried beans. Bake in middle of oven until golden, about 15 minutes. Let cool to room temperature and then chill for 1 hour in refrigerator.

Make the filling while the crust chills. In a bowl, using an electric mixer, beat mascarpone, sugar and vanilla together until smooth. Pour filling into chilled crust, spreading evenly, and arrange raspberries on top.

If keeping the tart longer than a day, brush raspberries lightly with a glaze of warmed apple jelly.

**Tip**
When out picking raspberries in your yard or favorite U-pick farm, keep them as cool as possible (ideally, pick them during cooler times of the day or on a cloudy day), and store them unwashed.

*Raspberries are healthy, antioxidant-rich berries high in ellagic acid—the same family of tannins that make wine, green tea and fruit such as pomegranates an important part of a healthy lifestyle.*

# Fruit Smoothie

## Serves 1

Fruit smoothies may never overtake coffee as Washington's morning beverage of choice, yet they are hands-down the healthiest and tastiest breakfast beverage for people on the go. Smoothies are the perfect excuse (although who needs one?) to use some of Washington's yummiest fruits—local blueberries, red-all-the-way-through strawberries, and organic peaches from Pence Orchards in Wapato. For an incredible treat, use some frozen huckleberries in your next smoothie. Take them right from the freezer into the blender. Smoothies can also be made using frozen yogurt, frozen bananas, ice cream or even soy milk. Try a shot of Baileys Irish Cream in a chocolate banana smoothie for a weekend indulgence.

1 banana, peeled,
cut and frozen
¾ cup fresh or frozen berries
¼ cup coconut milk
1 cup vanilla soy milk
1 Tbsp almond butter
¼ cup crushed ice

Purée all ingredients in a blender until smooth.

**Tip**
Coconut milk from a can will keep in the fridge for 4 to 5 days.

*Add some flax seed or bran for a really healthy kick.*

# Blackberry Wine

### Makes about 12 bottles

Ask a Seattleite to name one of the most invasive weeds in our area and you're likely to hear *Rubus discolor*, more commonly known as the Himalayan blackberry. Strangely though, our community has collective amnesia about this creeping blight in our parks and backyards come August when the fruit ripens. Children clamor to pick them. Adults make pies, and some make wine. Perhaps it's just another form of making lemonade out of lemons. If the other most invasive species in this area (English Ivy) could be made into a wine, you can be sure it would. Not feeling like making your own blackberry wine? Try Eagle Haven Winery's hand at it. Located outside of Sedro-Woolley, their wine is made from the 2000 pounds of blackberries picked from their property.

**8 cups blackberries**
**16 cups boiling water**
**10 cups granulated sugar**
**4 cups prunes**

Put berries into a large container that will not react to acids. Bring water to a boil and pour over berries. Let sit for 2 days, stirring occasionally. Strain. Stir in sugar.

Boil this mixture for 5 minutes, then add prunes. Place in a large crock, cover with cheesecloth and let sit for 2 months. Strain and bottle.

Age bottles at least 6 months before drinking.

**Variation**
You can also make this recipe with blueberries instead of blackberries.

# Heirloom Tomato Salad

**Serves 4**

Heirloom tomatoes are often gnarled, bumpy and deeply grooved. Don't for a moment be put off by their imperfect looks; their flavor will make you quickly convert to using them as often as possible. Heirloom tomatoes come from seeds collected by growers committed to preserving the diversity of tomatoes. Some heirloom cultivars have been handed down among family members for generations.

**1 clove garlic, minced**

**splash of white balsamic vinegar (see p. 6)**

**¼ cup olive oil**

**sea salt and freshly ground pepper to taste**

**1 lb heirloom tomatoes, washed, cored and sliced ½ inch thick**

**½ lb bocconcini, sliced the same thickness as the tomatoes**

**handful of fresh basil leaves, washed and patted dry**

**French baguette**

Place the garlic, vinegar and oil in a salad bowl, then add the tomatoes, tossing gently to coat with dressing. Season to taste with salt and pepper.

On individual plates, layer tomato slices with bocconcini slices, and tuck some basil in between and around. Scatter remaining basil leaves on top and drizzle with dressing remaining in salad bowl.

Serve with slices of crusty French baguette.

**Tip**
Fresh tomatoes from the garden or the farmers' market would also work in this recipe.

The classic combination of tomatoes, bocconcini and basil is known as a Caprese Salad, after the Isle of Capri in Italy. Purists would leave out the garlic and the balsamic vinegar from our recipe —try it both ways and decide which is more to your taste. One thing is certain, however: to bring out the fullest flavor, make sure you allow all your ingredients to come to room temperature before making this salad.

# Apple and Quinoa Salad

### Serves 6 as a main-course salad

Our state is responsible for producing more than half of all the apples grown in the United States. Washington apples are sold in all 50 states and in more than 40 countries around the world. Our new favorite apple is a toss-up between the easy-eating Gala, a mild, sweet, small variety, and the Honeycrisp, one of the best fresh eating apples out there. The Honeycrisp is so fantastically juicy it often reminds us of biting into a piece of watermelon. Honeycrisp is best eaten out of hand or in a salad such as this one (the high water content makes it a poor choice for baking). By pairing local apples from a farm such as BelleWood Acres (with 24,000 Jonagold and Honeycrisp trees) with quinoa, which is a seed from a plant in the same family as spinach and buckwheat, you can offer your guests an incredibly healthy and tasty salad. Quinoa is available in the grains section of large grocery stores and health food stores across Washington.

**juice from 1 lemon**

**⅓ cup apple cider vinegar**

**½ cup orange juice**

**⅓ cup canola
or sunflower oil**

**⅓ cup honey**

**5 cups cooked quinoa**

**2 Honeycrisp or Gala
apples, cored and chopped**

**1 bell pepper, diced small**

**1 cup fresh corn kernels**

**½ cup dried cranberries**

**½ cup currants**

**1 small red onion,
finely chopped**

**1 cup toasted, chopped
pecans (see Tip, p. 134)**

**1 cup each chopped fresh
parsley and mint**

**sea salt and freshly ground
pepper to taste**

Place lemon juice, apple cider vinegar, orange juice, oil and honey in a small bowl and stir to combine. Place cooked quinoa in a large bowl with all remaining ingredients. Combine well, then stir in dressing. Adjust seasonings and refrigerate until ready to serve.

To cook quinoa, bring 4 cups water to a boil in a wide-bottomed pot with a lid. Add a pinch of salt and stir in 2 cups quinoa. Reduce heat to a simmer, cover and cook until all the water is absorbed, about 25 minutes.

### Tip

You can cook any amount of quinoa you like as long as you keep the 2:1 ratio of liquid to grain. It is also worth experimenting with other liquids such as stock or coconut milk.

**Tip**
If there is any leftover quinoa, you can warm it up and
add a little cinnamon and cream for a nice breakfast.

# Artichoke and Fennel Strudels

## Serves 8 to 10 as an appetizer

Artichokes are thought to have originated in Sicily. Imagine how hungry some-one must have been to risk fighting the thorns and thistle of the artichoke that very first time. Luckily for us, the intrepid eater forged onward. Eating an arti-choke is often a lesson in enjoying the journey as well as the destination, and the work to procure the heart takes a little time. The leaves are delicious dipped in butter and lemon or in a sauce made with citrus juice, olive oil, garlic and herbs. Here, we are pairing delectable slices of the heart with the licorice-flavored fen-nel bulb, rendered mellow and sweet with some cooking. Both vegetables are then cloaked in a blanket of puff pastry with local goat cheese. Because the filling can be made a day ahead and we use ready-to-bake puff pastry, this recipe would be a great appetizer to make for your next dinner party (the filling can easily be doubled to serve more guests)—or serve it as a lunch with a salad of greens.

**1 Tbsp grape seed oil**

**½ medium white onion, diced into ¼-inch pieces**

**½ bulb fennel, outer leaves removed, sliced thinly**

**1 medium-large artichoke**

**juice from 1 lemon**

**⅛ cup sliced sundried tomatoes**

**½ cup water**

**sea salt and freshly ground pepper**

**1 package of puff pastry, thawed according to package directions**

**2 oz soft goat cheese**

**2 eggs, lightly beaten**

Heat oil over medium-low in a medium saucepan, and add onion and fennel. Cook, stirring occasion-ally, until light golden brown, about 10 minutes.

Meanwhile, prepare the artichoke. Snap off the dark outer leaves then slice off the cone. Cut or break off the stem, leaving just the bottom. Use a melon baller to scrape out the choke. Rub cut surfaces with lemon juice right away, as arti-chokes oxidize very quickly. Slice thinly and coat with lemon juice again.

Add sliced artichoke heart to the pan and cook, stirring occasionally, until they begin to color, about 5 minutes. Increase heat to medium, add sundried tomatoes and water, and cook, stir-ring occasionally, until the pan is almost dry and the artichoke hearts are tender. Remove from heat, season to taste with salt and pepper, and set aside to cool completely. (The recipe can be done a day ahead up to this point.)

Preheat oven to 400° F. Roll one sheet of puff pastry out into a 12 x 15-inch rectangle. With a sharp knife, cut into 10 rectangles (6 x 3 inches each).

Place 2 Tbsp of filling in the center of every second rectangle. Top with a couple of dots of goat cheese. Brush the edges of each rectangle with beaten egg and top with a second rectangle of puff pastry. Crimp the edges with a fork. Transfer to a parchment-lined baking sheet. Repeat with the second sheet of puff pastry. Brush tops of strudels with beaten egg. Bake until puffed and golden, about 25 to 30 minutes.

# Mushroom Soup with Parsley Oil

**Serves 6**

What are you looking for if you are with slightly secretive, highly enthusiastic and perhaps eccentric folks scampering over the forest floors and open areas of Washington's diverse landscape? Ah, you must be on an age-old search for the elusive wild mushroom under the tutelage of a pro. The locations of the "best spots" for mushroom hunting are rarely disclosed, even within the family. Today, the prized selections for both commercial and home foragers include morels, chanterelles, lobster and pine mushrooms. Most folks in Seattle have bumped into Jeremy Faber's Foraged and Found Edibles at any of the farmers' markets where he peddles his perfectly fresh wild harvest. It is through him that we learned all about man-on-horseback mushroom, angel's wings and the highly prized bolete (known as porcini in Italy).

**3 cups evenly sliced fresh, cleaned wild mushrooms, such as chanterelles, lobster or morels**

**2 Tbsp olive oil**

**¼ cup unsalted butter**

**1 large yellow onion, diced**

**2 large Yukon Gold potatoes, diced**

**¼ cup dry sherry**

**1 *bouquet garni* of parsley, thyme and bay leaf**

**3 dried juniper berries, bruised**

**4 cloves garlic, minced**

**8 cups chicken or vegetable stock**

**1 cup heavy cream (32 percent)**

Sauté mushrooms in batches in a large pot with olive oil and half of butter until nicely browned. Remove mushrooms and set aside. In same pot, melt remaining butter and add onions and potatoes. Sauté until golden, then deglaze with sherry. Add *bouquet garni*, juniper berries, garlic, mushrooms and stock. Bring to a boil, then immediately reduce heat to a simmer and cook until liquid has reduced by a third.

Add cream, bring almost to a boil and remove from heat. Remove *bouquet garni*. Purée soup in a blender until smooth. Serve hot, garnished with Parsley Oil (see opposite).

*A bouquet garni is a small bundle of herbs used to flavor stocks and soups. The ingredients vary depending on the dish, but the basic version is a sprig each of parsley and thyme and one bay leaf, all tied together for easy removal from the soup before serving.*

### Parsley Oil

Combine parsley and oil in a medium saucepan over medium heat until the oil begins to sputter. Set aside to cool to room temperature. Purée the mixture in a blender, then let sit for 1 hour. Strain the mixture through a double layer of large coffee filters wrapped in cheesecloth. Allow plenty of time to strain the mixture; do not press on the solids or you risk making the oil cloudy. Store in the fridge up to 2 weeks.

**1½ bunches of fresh parsley, chopped**

**1 cup grape seed oil**

### Tip

If fresh wild mushrooms are not available, use half the quantity of dried wild mushrooms. Reconstitute them in a bowl of hot water or stock for about 10 minutes—add enough liquid to cover and use a small plate to keep them submerged. Save the liquid to add to your soup; it will be full of great mushroom flavor.

### Warning

Because some mushrooms contain deadly toxins, eat only mushrooms positively identified as edible.

# Lentil and Roasted Garlic Soup

## Serves 4 to 6

Lentils are in the group of plants known as pulses or legumes, where the seed is grown in a pod; other examples are chickpeas and beans. Lentils are one of our favorite legumes because of their short cooking time and high protein and fiber concentrations. Washington state leads the nation, producing over a third of the total U.S. production. The humble lentil is celebrated annually at the National Lentil Festival (lentil ice cream, anyone?). Located in the Palouse region in eastern Washington, Pullman plays host to this celebration, proud of the 135 million pounds of lentils grown right in its backyard every year. Under blue skies and intense summer sun, the lentils dry naturally on their vines, combines harvest them and then the seeds are separated, sorted and sent all over the world.

½ tsp cinnamon

¼ tsp cloves

1 Tbsp cumin

2 tsp olive oil

1 cup chopped onions

½ cup diced carrot

1 large bay leaf

½ inch piece of fresh ginger, peeled and chopped

2 cups dried red lentils, rinsed

water

1 bulb roasted garlic (see p. 151), cloves squeezed out

1 Tbsp apple cider vinegar

2 tsp chopped cilantro

sea salt and freshly ground pepper to taste

finely sliced chives for garnish

In a small pan, toast the cinnamon, cloves and cumin until very fragrant, about 1 to 2 minutes. Set aside.

In a medium pot, heat oil over medium-high and sauté onions until translucent. Add carrot, bay leaf, ginger and toasted cinnamon mixture, and sauté about 2 minutes. Add lentils and enough water to cover by 1 inch and cook 30 to 45 minutes, or until the lentils are completely soft. Purée lentils and the roasted garlic in a blender. Stir in the apple cider vinegar and cilantro. Season with salt and plenty of pepper. Garnish each serving with chives.

Lentils are practically folic acid pills: 1 cup provides 90 percent of the recommended daily allowance. There is more folic acid in lentils that in any other unfortified food.

# Spiced Parsnip and Cauliflower Soup

## Serves 4 to 6

With its elegant ivory color and sweet, complex flavor, the parsnip is the queen of root vegetables. It can be used in everything from soups to main courses. When combined with some melted butter and brown sugar, honey or maple syrup for a side dish, it tastes just like candy. In season from September to February, parsnips are best eaten late in autumn, once they have benefited from exposure to frost. Strangely, parsnips have either flown under the radar completely or they produce a nose-wrinkling response from those who remember eating them raw or undercooked. Parsnips are completely different when allowed to cook slowly; they are even better when allowed to caramelize, giving off a heavenly scent of equal parts earth, nut and sugar.

2 to 3 Tbsp olive oil

1 Tbsp yellow mustard seeds

2 onions, finely chopped

2 cloves garlic, minced

1 tsp finely chopped fresh ginger

1 Tbsp turmeric

1 tsp cardamom

1 tsp cumin

1 lb cauliflower, trimmed and cut into florets

1 lb parsnips, peeled and cut into chunks roughly the same size as the cauliflower

2 cups vegetable or chicken stock or water

1⅔ cups coconut milk

sea salt and freshly ground pepper to taste

1 Tbsp finely chopped fresh cilantro

Place the oil in a large saucepan and heat over medium-high. When the oil is hot, add the mustard seeds and cook until they begin to pop. Add the onion, garlic and ginger, and cook for a couple of minutes until the onion is soft and translucent. Add turmeric, cardamom and cumin. Add cauliflower and parsnip and cook the mixture while stirring for a couple of minutes. Add the stock or water to the pan and bring it slowly to a boil. Skim off any scum that comes to the top and reduce the soup to a simmer. Leave it to cook gently for 30 minutes, stirring regularly.

The soup is ready when the cauliflower is cooked and tender. Stir in the coconut milk. Purée the soup in a blender until smooth and return it to a clean saucepan. Season the soup with salt and pepper, garnish with cilantro and serve.

## Tip
Parsnips are best stored in a very cold location or in the refrigerator.

*For a different snack, try making parsnip chips! With a sharp vegetable peeler, peel 3 or 4 parsnips lengthwise into long paper-thin strips, until you've reached the central core. Heat 1 to 2 inches of oil in a medium-sized saucepan to 350° F. Drop in parsnip strips in small batches and fry for 1 minute until crisp and golden. Drain on paper towels, season with sea salt and serve.*

# Pumpkin Fondue

### Serves 12 as an appetizer

Rummage through your parents' garage, or perhaps your own, and you are bound to find a fondue pot given as a wedding gift in the 1970s. Three decades later, fondues have come back in vogue, so go and dust it off and fire it up. There are endless variations of fondue these days, including this novel take on the more traditional cheese fondue. An oil or broth can be used for meat fondues, and chocolate fondue is another popular version usually using fruit or angel food cake for dipping. There's nothing like an edible bowl to leave a lasting impression on your guests—just don't dig too enthusiastically into the tender pumpkin flesh or you'll create an unanticipated fondue river on the table.

1 sugar pumpkin, about 3 to 4 lbs

2 Tbsp unsalted butter

1 small onion, finely chopped

1 clove garlic, minced

1 cup dry white wine

pinch of freshly grated nutmeg

2 Tbsp flour

¼ cup chopped fresh sage

2 cups grated aged white Cheddar cheese

½ cup sour cream

sea salt and freshly ground pepper to taste

Preheat oven to 350° F. Pierce the top of the pumpkin with a knife 3 or 4 times and bake for 20 minutes. Let cool for 10 minutes. Remove the top a quarter of the way down the pumpkin to form a lid. Scoop out the seeds and fibers and set aside. Increase oven temperature to 375° F.

Melt butter in a medium saucepan and sauté onion for 5 minutes. Add garlic and cook until softened. Add white wine and bring to a simmer. Finally, add nutmeg, flour, sage and cheese and stir until the cheese is melted. Pour into the pumpkin, cover with its lid and bake for 20 minutes, until the mixture is hot. Remove from oven and stir in sour cream. Adjust salt and pepper, if needed, and serve with skewers of crusty bread for dipping and spoons for scooping out the delicious pumpkin flesh.

# Slow-roasted Salmon with Columbia Valley Wine Sauce and Seared Boletus Mushrooms

### Serves 8

What could speak more favorably of the bounty of the Northwest than a recipe highlighting three of its greatest treasures from sea, land and mountains: salmon from our cold Pacific waters, a lovely sauce made with a red wine blend from the Columbia Valley in eastern Washington and wild boletus mushrooms (also known as porcini) foraged in the mountains.

**Sauce**

2 medium shallots, rough chopped

1 tsp fennel seeds, lightly crushed with the side of a knife

1 star anise pod

2 tsp honey

1 bottle of red wine blend from Columbia Valley (such as JM Cellars Bramble Bump Red or Dunham Cellars 3 Legged Red)

4 cups vegetable or low-sodium chicken stock

2 sticks unsalted butter, cut into pieces

fennel fronds (optional, for garnish)

Preheat oven to 250° F. In a wide saucepan, combine the shallots, fennel seeds, star anise, honey, red wine and stock. Bring to a boil then reduce the heat to a gentle simmer. Reduce the sauce until you have 2 cups (30 to 40 minutes).

Lay the salmon pieces on a parchment-lined baking sheet. Rub salmon with olive oil and sprinkle with salt. Slow roast for 10 to 12 minutes. The salmon is done when it just barely flakes. It is best served on the rare side. Keep warm, covered with foil, while you finish the sauce and cook the mushrooms.

Heat a large pan over medium-high. Add the butter and olive oil. Add the mushrooms and sear until browned, about 2 to 3 minutes. Flip the pieces over and sear the other sides. Add a little water to the pan if mushrooms stick. Cook until tender, about 8 to 10 minutes total.

Finish the sauce by straining it through a fine mesh sieve. Return the sauce to the saucepan over medium-low heat. Whisk the butter into the sauce a little at a time and keep warm over very low heat.

Spoon a small amount of sauce onto each plate, top with a piece of salmon, and scatter mushrooms over all. Garnish with fennel fronds.

### Salmon

2 lbs wild King salmon, skinned, bones removed and cut into 8 equal portions

2 Tbsp extra virgin olive oil

2 generous pinches of fine sea salt

### Boletus Mushrooms

1 Tbsp butter

1 Tbsp extra virgin olive oil

1 lb wild boletus mushrooms, wiped with a damp paper towel if dirty and sliced into ¼-inch slices

sea salt and freshly ground pepper to taste

# Coq au Vin with Bergevin Lane Calico Red

### Serves 6

In 1825, Washington's first recorded wine grapes were planted by the Hudson's Bay Company at Fort Vancouver. Since that moment, the growth of the wine industry in this region has exploded forth, growing exponentially each and every year. Pity the poor Washington wine drinker who just can't decide which of the 100-plus—and growing all the time—wineries to visit in the Walla Walla Valley. Luckily for us, we stumbled upon Bergevin Lane's easy-drinking Calico Red. It's a blend of Cabernet Sauvignon, Syrah, Merlot, Cab Franc and Zinfandel, and it has lush dark and red berry flavors and aromas, with a hint of spice. It is both a great value (priced under $20) and an ideal wine to slowly perfume the meat in this braised dish. While many people think of Coq au Vin as a dish using red wine, it is actually meant to be a dish using the "local" wine (red or white), so many regions of France have variations of the dish—even Coq au Champagne. Walla Walla and Bordeaux share the same latitude, so it's not a stretch to sip some wine (buy two bottles) and feel somehow connected to our friends in France while your dinner slowly cooks.

2 Tbsp unsalted butter

²⁄₃ cup diced bacon

1 x 3 to 4 lb free-range chicken, cut into 8 pieces

2 medium onions, chopped

1 carrot, chopped

1 cup celery root, diced

2 cloves garlic, sliced

2 Tbsp flour

1 bottle of Bergevin Lane Calico Red

4 sprigs of fresh thyme

8 cups chicken stock

3 bay leaves

¼ cup unsalted butter

2 cups small white button mushrooms, left whole

sea salt and freshly ground pepper

Melt the butter in heavy-bottomed casserole and add the bacon. Cook over medium heat until bacon is crisp, drain it on paper towels and place in a large bowl.

Season the chicken pieces with salt and pepper and cook them in the bacon drippings until they are golden brown. Transfer to the bowl with the bacon. Add the onions, carrot and celery root to the pan and cook slowly on medium heat, stirring from time to time, until the onion is translucent. Add the garlic and stir in the flour; let cook for 3 to 5 minutes. Add the chicken, bacon, red wine, thyme and enough chicken stock to cover the chicken. Bring to a boil, reduce heat and cook, partially covered, for 45 minutes to 1 hour or until the chicken is tender.

Meanwhile, melt the remaining butter in a small pan and sauté the mushrooms until golden. Season them lightly with salt and pepper, and add to the chicken. To serve, ladle some of the sauce into a saucepan and reduce over high heat until thick and glossy. Serve the chicken and sauce over hot buttered noodles.

**Tip**
Blended wines are a particularly good choice for wine sauces or long cooking braises because the inherent balance that the varietals contribute to the mix stays consistent when the wine is reduced down to its essence.

*This classic French dish is hearty and rich, with local chicken and fragrant herbs stewed in red wine. Age is definitely a virtue—in this recipe, using an older bird produces a richer flavor.*

# Apple-roasted Pheasant

## Serves 4

Apples and pheasant together make the perfect fall dish to celebrate a successful growing season. The sweet and earthy flavor notes of cinnamon and cloves will penetrate the meat of the pheasant in its quick roast in the oven. For extra flavor, you could also roast the pheasant on your barbecue and use some apple wood chips under the grate to add some smoky apple notes to the dish. This recipe can also be made with other poultry such as quail or chicken, and you could even experiment with other local fruits such as quince or pears. As with quail, it may be a bit of a search to find local pheasant. Entrepreneurs take note: the market is ripe for a commercial small game producer to start a business in Washington.

4 pheasant breasts, skin on, wing attached

sea salt and freshly ground black pepper

1 Tbsp butter

1 Tbsp grape seed oil or olive oil

4 cups peeled and sliced Pink Lady apples

¼ cup honey

1 Tbsp minced garlic

1 tsp cinnamon

1 tsp cloves

juice from ½ lemon

Preheat oven to 425° F. Season pheasant with salt and pepper. Heat butter and oil in an oven-proof sauté pan that is large enough to comfortably fit all the meat. On medium-high heat, sear pheasant breasts, skin side down, for 3 to 4 minutes until golden brown. Set aside.

Combine all the remaining ingredients in a mixing bowl and sauté in the same pan as the pheasant. When the apples are nicely caramelized, about 5 minutes, place the pheasant on top, skin sides up, and roast in the oven for 10 to 12 minutes, until the meat is cooked through. To serve, place a spoonful of the caramelized apples on each plate and top with a pheasant breast.

Native to Japan and China, the pheasant is a member of the Phasianidae family of birds, which includes the quail and the peacock. Terrestrial birds that can be distinguished by the male's ornate plumage, pheasants were introduced in North America in 1881.

# Silky Chicken Curry

### Serves 6

While Washington doesn't have a large Indian population, there are still communities in Renton, Kent, Seattle, Bellevue, Marysville, Bellingham and Spokane. For dining, people swear by Preets in Redmond, while Punjap Sweets in Kent is noteworthy for its marvelous Indian pastries and sugary treats. Folks willing to venture further afield should make the short trip over the border, as neighboring British Columbia is reputed to have excellent Indian cuisine.

¼ cup unsalted butter

3 medium onions, finely diced

3 cloves garlic, minced

1 Tbsp grated fresh ginger

⅓ cup curry paste

2 tsp freshly ground cumin

pinch of cayenne or chili powder (optional)

2½ lbs diced chicken or 1 x 4 lb chicken, cut into 10 pieces

2 medium carrots, peeled and diagonally sliced

1 red pepper, diced

1 medium tomato, diced

1 cup coconut milk

sea salt and freshly ground pepper

fresh cilantro, chopped

1 cup toasted and chopped unsalted cashews (see Tip, p. 134)

Melt butter over medium heat in a wide, heavy-bottomed pot. Add onions, garlic and ginger and cook about 5 minutes. Stir in curry paste, cumin and cayenne and cook 2 minutes. Add chicken, stirring to coat, then add carrots, red pepper, tomato and coconut milk.

Bring to a simmer, cover and cook about 30 minutes, or until chicken is cooked. Season with salt and pepper. Curry can be made up to 3 days in advance and refrigerated.

Serve curry hot, garnished with cilantro and cashews, accompanied by basmati or jasmine rice and a side of plain yogurt or raita (see opposite).

## Raita

Peel, seed and grate cucumbers into a colander and let drain 15 minutes. Transfer grated cucumber to a bowl, squeezing out as much moisture as possible, then stir in yogurt, mint, cumin, salt and pepper. Store, refrigerated, for up to 5 days.

**2 long English cucumbers**
**1 cup plain yogurt**
**¼ cup chopped fresh mint**
**ground cumin, sea salt and freshly ground pepper to taste**

## Tip

If you fear cooking rice (and don't have an electric rice cooker), try this foolproof method. Cook your rice as you would cook pasta, in a big pot of boiling, salted water. Check rice often for doneness, then drain in a fine mesh colander and serve. This method is especially suited to cooking large quantities of rice.

# Duck Confit with Caramelized Rutabaga and Risotto

## Serves 10

In this recipe we have chosen to incorporate one of our favorite fall vegetables, rutabagas. Rutabagas are believed to have originated as a hybrid of turnips and wild cabbage. Caramelizing these humble roots brings out their natural sweetness and accentuates their complex earthiness. Duck confit is simply duck that has been salt cured and poached in its own fat until it is very tender. There is something sinfully delicious about the rich, savory quality of good duck confit. If you don't have time to make it yourself, you can often find it in Seattle supermarkets such as Metropolitan Market, or you can order it over the Internet.

**10 duck legs**

**2 heads of garlic, halved crosswise**

**1 lemon, sliced into about 5 rings**

**1 orange, sliced into about 5 rings**

**½ cinnamon stick**

**4 star anise, whole**

**1 tsp black peppercorns, whole**

**½ inch piece of fresh ginger, sliced into 3 pieces**

**6 sprigs of fresh thyme**

**3 bay leaves**

**½ lb kosher salt**

**about 2 lbs of rendered duck fat**

**4 cups grape seed or olive oil**

### Carmelized Rutabaga

**2 Tbsp butter**

**2 Tbsp brown sugar**

**2 small rutabaga, peeled, quartered and sliced ¼ inch thick**

**sea salt and freshly ground pepper to taste**

Layer the duck legs, garlic halves, lemon and orange slices, spices and herbs, in a nonreactive container, generously sprinkling with salt between each layer. Cover with plastic wrap, and cure in refrigerator for 24 hours.

Preheat the oven to 250° F. Remove the duck legs and pat them dry (you can rinse them if you prefer a milder salt flavor). Rinse and drain garlic, fruit, spices and herbs. Place duck legs and fruit mixture, alternating layers, into a deep baking dish and cover with the duck fat and oil. Bake for 6 to 8 hours or until the meat is very tender. The duck is ready to serve hot or it can be cooled and preserved in a crock or plastic container in the refrigerator for up to 3 months. If storing, strain the fat through a fine sieve and pour enough over the meat to cover.

Fir the rutabaga, eat butter and brown sugar in a small pan until butter is melted. Add rutabaga slices and cook over medium heat until tender, about 12 to 15 minutes. Season with salt and pepper and set aside.

### Risotto

Melt butter in a skillet over medium heat and sauté onion until softened but not colored, about 5 minutes. Add the rice and sauté for 2 to 4 minutes, stirring to coat the grains. Then add the white wine, stir to combine until it is absorbed, about 3 minutes. Add a ladle of the hot broth, stirring slowly but continuously, until it is almost completely absorbed by the rice. Continue adding broth until all of it is absorbed and the rice is tender but slightly chewy and very creamy, about 25 minutes. Stir in the remaining tablespoon of butter and the parsley and Parmesan cheese. Add salt and pepper to taste. Serve the risotto piping hot with the duck confit and caramelized rutabaga.

¼ cup unsalted butter,
plus 1 Tbsp to finish

¼ cup chopped onion

2 cups Arborio rice

½ cup white wine

5 cups hot chicken or vegetable broth

¼ cup chopped fresh parsley

½ cup grated Parmesan cheese

sea salt and freshly ground
pepper to taste

# Grilled Quail with Pistachio and Pomegranate

### Serves 4

Quail belongs to a family of game birds that were vital to the survival of both native peoples and early settlers. Most quail used for food consumption these days are raised in captivity. Known for their rich, moist meat, quail are the most popular of the small-game birds. While quail are frequently offered on the menus of upscale restaurants, they are also available in specialty shops and meat markets for the home cook. Encourage your guests to put away forks and knives; the best way to enjoy quail is by picking it up with your hands and eating it right off the bone. As of this writing, we are not aware of a local source for quail, so encourage your local farmer to start up a small operation!

**4 quail, cut through back-bone and flattened out**

**sea salt and freshly ground pepper**

### Marinade

**½ clove garlic, minced**

**1 tsp cinnamon**

**1 tsp cumin**

**½ onion, finely chopped**

**3 Tbsp pomegranate molasses (see opposite)**

**juice from ½ lime**

### Sauce

**1 cup diced bacon**

**½ clove garlic, minced**

**¼ cup pomegranate molasses**

**½ cup whole pistachios**

**sea salt and freshly ground pepper to taste**

**arugula leaves for garnish**

In a large bowl, prepare marinade and toss to combine. Season each quail with salt and pepper and place in marinade. Cover and refrigerate for at least 1 hour and up to 24 hours.

For the sauce, sauté bacon in a pan until crispy. Remove all the fat drippings except for 1 Tbsp. Add garlic and sauté until fragrant, about 1 minute. Add remaining ingredients and heat through.

Grill quail over medium-high heat for about 7 minutes each side, or until juices run clear. Serve on a bed of arugula leaves with sauce drizzled on top.

**Tip**

Another delicious way to cook these birds is to wrap them in grape leaves. If you have fresh leaves, blanch them first in boiling water for a few seconds. Pat dry and remove the stalks. If you are using preserved leaves, rinse them well and pat dry. Rub the quail with olive oil and season with salt and pepper. Wrap the quail first in pancetta and then in the grape leaves. Grill until cooked through and enjoy immediately.

*Pomegranate molasses is syrup made from cooked-down pomegranate juice. It can be found in Middle Eastern stores, or order it over the Internet.*

# Sweet and Sour Pork

## Serves 6

Immigrants from China (mostly from the southeast) played a key role in the development of Washington as a whole. More than 3000 Chinese lived here by 1880, working to build western railroads and assisting in all aspects of our region's major industries. Chinese Americans, like many immigrant groups, faced open hostility and legal barriers from the majority white population for generations. Overcoming much adversity, Wing Luke was elected to the Seattle City Council in 1962, becoming the first Chinese American in the U.S. mainland to do so. Sweeping reforms in 1965 led to an explosion of new immigration. Seattle's Chinatown is in the heart of the International District (known as the I.D. locally). Here you can eat some of the best Chinese food to be found in Washington; from dim sum at SunYa to succulent barbecue duck hanging in the window at King's, to pastries at Mee Sum. Walking a four-block radius exposes you to a culinary tour best capped by a trip through Chinese history (and its vibrant present) at the well-respected Wing Luke Museum.

**2 Tbsp cornstarch**

**1 Tbsp cold water**

**1 lb boneless pork loin rib, cut into bite-sized pieces**

**2 egg yolks**

**1 Tbsp soy sauce**

**2 tsp sea salt**

**⅔ cup rice wine vinegar**

**¼ cup white wine**

**⅓ cup sugar**

**3 cloves garlic, minced**

**2 Tbsp grated fresh ginger**

**½ small pineapple, peeled, cored, quartered and sliced**

**1 small tomato, diced**

**½ cup julienned red pepper**

**1 tsp cinnamon**

**vegetable oil for frying**

**¼ cup each cornstarch and flour, sifted together into a bowl**

**1 cup snow peas**

In a bowl, add cornstarch to cold water and mix well. Add pork, egg yolks, soy sauce and 1 tsp salt. Toss well and refrigerate overnight.

Place vinegar, wine, sugar and remaining salt into a pan and bring to a boil. Add garlic and ginger; reduce heat and simmer for 10 minutes. Add pineapple, tomato, red pepper and cinnamon and simmer an additional 10 minutes or until tomato becomes incorporated into sauce. Remove from heat and set sauce aside.

Heat 1 to 2 inches of oil in a saucepan to 350° F. Toss marinated pork in flour and cornstarch mixture and fry in hot oil until cooked, about 5 minutes. Drain well on kitchen towel. Heat sauce through, adding snow peas just before serving. Spoon sauce over pork and serve with rice or noodles.

**Tip**
Try this recipe with other meats, such as chicken or beef, or with tofu.
The sauce can be made up to 3 days ahead; store it in the fridge.

# Grilled Williamson Beef Tenderloin with Sautéed Chanterelles

## Serves 4

The people at Williamson Farm, located in the Columbia River Plateau of eastern Washington, know how to keep their cattle happy. Most importantly, they feed them a diet of 100 percent grass (grain can make cattle sick, necessitating the use of antibiotics). Jerry Williamson and his family have been in the business for four generations since the 1920s. The Williamsons should be proud of their accomplishment: they are the largest year-round producer of 100 percent grass-fed beef on open pasture. When cooking 100 percent grass-fed beef (also known as "grass-finished" beef, as most cattle spend at least part of their lives eating grass), keep in mind that it is leaner than grain-fed beef and tends to cook faster. Using an instant-read thermometer helps alleviate any doubt about when it is done.

**4 beef tenderloin medallions, about 6 to 8 oz each**

**olive oil for brushing**

**2 tsp kosher salt**

**freshly ground pepper**

### Mushrooms

**1 to 2 Tbsp olive oil**

**3 shallots, sliced**

**1 lb fresh chanterelles**

**1 clove garlic, minced**

**½ cup white wine**

**1 cup chopped parsley**

**¼ cup chopped chives**

**sea salt and freshly ground pepper**

Remove beef medallions from refrigerator 15 minutes before cooking.

To prepare the mushrooms, place olive oil in a skillet over medium-high heat and sauté the shallots until soft. Add chanterelles and garlic and continue to sauté for 5 to 7 minutes, then add white wine and cook until the liquid evaporates. Remove from heat and stir in parsley and chives. Season with salt and pepper and set aside.

Heat a grill or a stovetop grill pan to medium-high. Brush beef lightly with olive oil, and season with salt and pepper. Cook medallions on the grill, without moving them around, until nice grill marks appear, about 4 minutes. Turn the medallions and continue to grill until an instant-read thermometer inserted into them sideways registers about 120° F, about 3 to 4 minutes more. Set aside on a cutting board to rest for 5 minutes before serving. To serve, divide medallions among 4 plates and spoon on the mushrooms.

# Coffee and Chocolate Braised Short Ribs

### Serves 6

Short ribs have not always been the darling staple of top restaurants. This cut of meat has lots of fat, meat, bone and connective tissue and was once considered "what was left" after the choice cuts of beef were taken. However, some simple kitchen magic entailing trimming and a long, moist cooking method results in meat that is tender, rich and flavorful. There are lots of short rib recipes calling for a wine-based braising liquid, but because Seattle has such a strong coffee culture, we felt some java would be an appropriate substitution. Use any good, strong coffee that is not too bitter and combine it with your favorite dark chocolate for a unique dish that will have your friends coming back for more!

¼ cup olive oil

5 lbs beef short ribs

salt and pepper

1 large onion, chopped

1 large red pepper, chopped

1 large jalapeño pepper, seeded and finely chopped

2 Tbsp brown sugar

1 tsp ancho chili powder

½ tsp oregano

1 tsp cumin

2 cups strong coffee

1 x 28 oz can of diced tomatoes in juice

1 Tbsp tomato paste

1 cup dark, unsweetened chocolate, at least 70 percent cocoa

sea salt and freshly ground pepper

chopped fresh cilantro

Preheat oven to 300° F. Place oil in a heavy-bottomed pot over medium-high heat. Season ribs with salt and pepper. Working in batches, sear short ribs in oil until nicely browned and transfer to a platter.

Reduce heat to medium and add onions and peppers to the oil and drippings in the pot, stirring until onions are translucent. Stir in garlic and sauté for 1 minute. Add brown sugar, ancho chili powder, cumin and oregano, and cook for 5 minutes. Stir in coffee, tomatoes and tomato paste, and bring the mixture to a boil. Add the short ribs and the collected juices to the pot and heat until boiling.

Cover and bake in oven until the meat is very tender, about 1¾ to 2 hours. Stir in chocolate until it is melted and evenly distributed in the sauce. Season to taste and garnish with cilantro. Serve with Smashed Yellow Finns with Fresh Herbs and Truffle Oil (see p. 108).

# Apple Cider-roasted Squash Ravioli with Brown Butter Hazelnut Sauce

### Serves 2 to 4

In 1928, John Victor Holmquist and his son, Anton, planted a hazelnut orchard that was the beginning of five generations of Holmquists farming the fertile soil in temperate northwest Washington. Holmquist Hazelnut Orchards grows the DuChilly hazelnut, a nut very different from the standard hazelnut you might be familiar with. DuChillys are a sweeter variety; they are long and thin and devoid of any bitterness commonly found in the round variety. Get in your car, drive up the I-5 corridor, look out the window at the changing leaves and stop in at Holmquist. You can even take home bags of the hazelnut shells to line your garden paths.

½ cup unsalted butter

½ small onion, diced

1 cup Apple Cider Butternut Squash Purée (see opposite)

sea salt and freshly ground pepper to taste

3 Tbsp heavy cream (32 percent)

3 Tbsp grated Parmesan cheese, plus more for topping

pinch of nutmeg

1 recipe pasta dough (p. 175), rolled out into wide ribbons

½ cup roughly chopped hazelnuts

1 Tbsp finely chopped fresh parsley leaves

In a large pan, melt 1 Tbsp of butter and sauté onion over medium heat. Add the butternut squash purée and cook until the mixture is slightly dry, about 2 to 3 minutes. Season with salt and pepper. Stir in cream and continue to cook for 2 minutes. Remove from the heat and stir in Parmesan cheese and nutmeg, and season with salt and pepper. Set the filling aside to cool completely.

Set a large pot of salted water to boil. Cut the pasta ribbons into 3-inch squares. Place 2 tsp of the filling in the center of each ravioli square. Using a pastry brush, lightly brush the edges of the pasta with water and cover with a second square. Press edges slightly to seal. If desired, you can cut the pasta into circles with a round cookie cutter. Add the ravioli to pot of boiling water and cook until *al dente*, about 2 to 3 minutes, or until they are paler in color and float to the surface. With a slotted spoon, remove the ravioli from the water and drain well.

In a large pan, melt the remaining butter over medium-high heat, add the hazelnuts and continue to cook until the butter starts to brown. Remove from the heat and toss ravioli in butter.

Place ravioli in the center of each serving plate and spoon any remaining butter sauce and hazelnuts on top. Sprinkle Parmesan cheese over the pasta and garnish with parsley.

### Apple Cider Butternut Squash Purée
Preheat oven to 375° F. Cut butternut squash in half lengthwise, scoop out seeds and place flesh side up on a baking pan. Pour apple cider on top, season lightly with salt and pepper and bake in oven for 45 minutes or until tender when pierced with a fork. Cool, scoop out flesh and mash.

**Apple Cider Buttenut Squash Purée**
**1 x 1 lb butternut squash**
**⅓ cup apple cider**
**sea salt and freshly ground pepper**

# Smashed Yellow Finn Potatoes with Fresh Herbs and Truffle Oil

**Serves 6**

Combining two great earthy ingredients—Washington potatoes (look for great ones from Olsen Farms out of Colville) and an aromatic oil infused with truffles—makes for a heavenly combination of flavors. Quality truffle oil is made by infusing good oil (usually olive), with luxurious Italian white or black truffles (make sure you avoid cheap synthetic truffle oils). The oil absorbs the aroma and flavor of the pungent fungi. Ordinary smashed potatoes become instantly layered with a complex earthiness. For extreme decadence, consider shaving some Oregon truffles right over the top just before serving. Use the truffle oil sparingly over local free-range eggs, with shavings of a hard aged cheese, or surprise your love with a bowl of truffle-laced popcorn the next time you watch a movie at home.

**2 lbs Yellow Finn potatoes**

**¼ cup sliced butter**

**3 Tbsp heavy cream (32 percent)**

**⅓ cup sour cream**

**¼ cup fresh herbs (use some of your favorites, such as thyme, rosemary, tarragon or dill)**

**truffle oil for drizzling**

**sea salt and freshly ground pepper to taste**

**thinly sliced green onion**

In a large pot, cover potatoes with salted water and bring to a boil over high heat. Reduce heat to medium-high and cook until the potatoes are tender when pricked with a fork, about 15 minutes. Drain, and return potatoes to pot.

Add butter and cream to the potatoes, and smash potatoes into uneven chunks with a large fork or potato masher. Mix in sour cream and fresh herbs, and season with salt and pepper. Drizzle truffle oil on top of the potatoes, sprinkle with green onion and serve.

# Jerusalem Artichoke Gratin
## Serves 4 to 6

Also known as "sunchokes," Jerusalem artichokes are easy to grow here (Washington is one of the leading commercial producing areas) and will even produce a display of small sunflowers late in the summer. In Washington, Jerusalem artichokes are best harvested in the fall when light frosts enhance their natural sweetness. A tuber native to North America, the Jerusalem artichoke has waxy flesh with the texture of a crispy apple and a flavor reminiscent of sunflower seeds. Traditionally, the tubers were simply boiled and eaten much like potatoes, and they can be used in place of potatoes in many recipes. In season from October to March, sunchokes can be eaten raw (sliced paper thin in salads or julienned in slaws) and they make excellent iron-rich soups.

**4 cloves garlic, chopped**

**2 1/2 Tbsp extra virgin olive oil**

**1 1/2 lbs Jerusalem artichokes**

**sea salt and freshly ground pepper to taste**

**1 Tbsp chopped fresh parsley**

Preheat oven to 350° F. Heat garlic and oil in a small pot and cook until soft. Peel Jerusalem artichokes and cut into small chunks, dropping chunks into a bowl of acidulated water (see below) as you work. Put in a shallow roasting pan large enough to hold everything in one layer comfortably. Strain garlic from oil and pour oil over the chokes. Add salt and pepper and toss.

Bake in oven for about 20 minutes, stirring once or twice, until tender. Sprinkle parsley on top and serve as a side dish.

*Acidulated water is just water to which a little acid—normally lemon or lime juice or vinegar—has been added; 1/2 tsp per cup is enough. When you are peeling or cutting fruits or vegetables that discolor quickly when exposed to air, such as apples, Jerusalem artichokes, globe artichokes and salsify, place them in acidulated water to prevent browning. Acidulated water is also sometimes used for cooking.*

The Jerusalem artichoke has no ties to the famous Biblical city; the name simply comes from the English misunderstanding of the Italian word girasol, which means "sunflower."

# Brussels Sprouts with Pancetta and Pine Nuts

### Serves 6

Because they do well in cool climates, Brussels sprouts are perfectly suited to western Washington; they even improve in flavor, sweetness and tenderness if allowed to chill through the first few frosts. Brussels sprouts, like cauliflower, are actually a variety of cabbage. Because Brussels sprouts are often overcooked, they do not hold a place among the stars of the vegetable kingdom (nor at many dinner tables), which is a shame. This antipathy evidently goes far—there's a sign hanging at a produce stall at the famous Pike Place Market that calls Brussels sprouts "little green balls of death," a clear indication that someone was force fed overcooked sprouts from an early age. Try this recipe and convert a sprouts hater by stacking the deck with some locally fabulous pepper-rubbed pancetta from da Pino's in South Seattle.

**2 lbs Brussels sprouts**

**splash of olive oil**

**5 oz pancetta or prosciutto, diced**

**sea salt and freshly ground pepper to taste**

**½ cup pine nuts, toasted (see Tip)**

Preheat oven to 400° F. Slice the Brussels sprouts in half lengthwise, removing any loose outer leaves and trimming the bottom stems. Toss in olive oil and add pancetta or prosciutto, salt and pepper. Spread in a single layer on a baking sheet and bake for 20 to 30 minutes until pancetta or prosciutto is crispy. Stir occasionally, so the Brussels sprouts cook evenly. Toss with the pine nuts and another splash of olive oil, if desired.

Tip
To toast nuts and seeds, place in a dry frying pan and cook on low heat, stirring occasionally, until lightly golden.

*Pancetta is Italian bacon. Prosciutto is a type of Italian dry-cured meat, usually made from pork.*

# Oven-roasted Quince

**Serves 4**

Quince is a wonderful but little-known fruit in Washington. Known as "the golden apple," it is native to Persia and Greece, although it was the Greeks who first cultivated quince as we know it today. Many historical accounts of the apple are likely botanical cases of mistaken identity that actually refer to the quince. Quince grown in northern climates is inedible when raw because it is too sour and hard; however, once cooked whole or made into a paste, this fruit can be used in sauces, as an accompaniment to roasted meats or eaten like applesauce.

**2 large quince, peeled and halved**

**2 cups honey**

**2 cups water**

**½ cup orange juice**

**1 vanilla bean, halved and split**

**Cinnamon Ice Cream**

**2 cups best quality vanilla ice cream**

**2 Tbsp ground cinnamon**

Preheat oven to 275° F. Combine all ingredients in an ovenproof dish and bring to a boil on the stovetop. Cover with a piece of parchment paper and weigh down with a small plate. Bake in oven for 3 hours, turning once during cooking.

Remove from oven and let cool. Store quince refrigerated in the syrup for up to 6 months.

To serve, pour syrup into a small saucepan and reduce it until it becomes a deep red, then toss the quince in the syrup to coat. Serve with Cinnamon Ice Cream.

**Cinnamon Ice Cream**
In an electric mixer or food processor, combine ice cream with cinnamon, then freeze until set.

Vanilla beans can be used to infuse sugar with a wonderful aroma and flavor. Cut a vanilla bean in half lengthwise (or dry and reuse the pods from the recipe) and cover with 1 to 2 cups of white sugar for 3 to 4 weeks or more, stirring once a week. You can use vanilla sugar in your coffee or tea, or add it to whipped cream.

# Onion Jam

Foodies in Seattle love chutneys and jams that pair well with cheese plates, roasted meats and more, and this recipe is perfect for all these applications. The caramelized flavor of this jam comes from a long cooking process, which brings out the sugars in the onion and causes them to caramelize. For this recipe, we have paired it with a cheese tray as part of an after-dinner treat, but it works equally well as an appetizer or even spooned on top of grilled scallops.

¼ cup olive oil

6 medium sweet onions, sliced thinly

pinch of sea salt

1 Tbsp balsamic vinegar

¼ cup Port wine

sprig of fresh thyme

½ cup muscovado sugar

1 tsp mustard seeds

½ tsp red pepper flakes

¼ cup finely chopped tomato

Melt the oil in heavy frying pan. Add the onions and sauté until slightly brown. Season with salt. Reduce the heat and continue to cook, stirring constantly, until caramelized and tender. Add the remaining ingredients, except the tomato, and cook on low heat for 30 minutes, stirring occasionally. Add the tomato and cook for 15 more minutes. Let cool.

*Try onion jam on pizzas and sandwiches.*

Artisan cheese producers are making incredible products at dizzying rates, giving lucky Washingtonians a wealth of choices when it comes to finding quality cheeses to pair with this onion jam. Try Estrella's Black Creek Buttery, an Old World-style Cheddar made from raw cow's milk, as well as their Montesano, a blended cow and goat's milk Romano cheese aged 3 to 9 months. For a unique cow's milk cheese that ripens from the outside in, pick up some of Mt. Townsend Creamery's Seastack, gently aged with an ash coating and an anointment of sea salt.

# Apple Cranberry Cinnamon Buns

## Makes 12

Cinnamon rolls are a North American and Northern European tradition, with entire stores in malls now dedicated to selling these sweet, sticky pastries. However, the best cinnamon rolls are the ones that come straight out of your oven, filling your home with the incomparable homeyness of baked bread and cinnamon. This variation of the traditional roll incorporates two abundant Washington state fruits: apples (we use the tart Granny Smith in this recipe) and cranberries (grown in bogs along the coast). Their tartness will counter all the sugar and icing these delicious morsels contain. Served warm on a Sunday morning, they make the perfect weekend brunch treat.

### Dough

¼ **cup warm water**

1 **Tbsp active dry yeast**

¼ **cup sugar**

2¼ **cups flour**

½ **cup buttermilk at room temperature**

1 **tsp salt**

2 **large egg yolks**

¼ **cup unsalted butter, softened**

### Filling

½ **cup dried cranberries**

2 **Granny Smith apples, peeled and chopped**

⅓ **cup brown sugar**

1 **tsp cinnamon**

1 **tsp cardamom**

2 **Tbsp unsalted butter, melted and cooled slightly**

Sprinkle yeast over warm water with 1 tsp sugar and let stand until foamy, 5 to 10 minutes. Add remaining sugar, flour, buttermilk, salt and yolks, and stir until everything is combined well. Transfer mixture to an electric mixer with a dough hook and beat in butter, a few pieces at a time, on medium speed until smooth and elastic, about 5 minutes. Scrape dough from side of bowl, cover bowl with plastic wrap and put in a warm place for 1 hour or until dough has doubled in size.

In a small bowl, stir together cranberries with the apples. In another bowl, stir together sugar, cinnamon and cardamom.

Grease a 9 x 13-inch baking pan. Transfer dough onto a floured surface and roll out into a 16 x 12-inch rectangle. Brush dough with melted butter, leaving an unbuttered 1/2-inch border on long sides. Sprinkle fruit filling evenly over the buttered area and then sprinkle cinnamon-cardamom sugar evenly over the filling. Roll up the shorter side of the dough, like a jelly roll, and pinch to seal the edge firmly. Cut into 12 even pieces and arrange, cut sides down, in the baking pan. Cover loosely with plastic wrap and let the buns rise in a warm place for 45 to 50 minutes or until they have doubled in size.

While buns are rising, preheat oven to 350° F. Bake buns in middle of oven until golden, about 25 minutes. Transfer buns to a rack and cool slightly before serving.

*Since 1999, Sweden has celebrated National Cinnamon Bun Day on October 4.*

# Gingered Pear Tarte Tatin
## Serves 8

Washington state is best known for its apples. However, fresh pear production here is the largest in the United States, with most of the orchards located in the Yakima and Wenatchee valleys. D'Anjou, Bartlett and Bosc are common varieties easily available in markets. Worth searching for is the small, sweet Seckel pear. For this pear tarte, look for flour from Stone-Buhr, which is the first flour company to buy locally grown flour and mill it in Spokane for local distribution. The cultivation practices of the wheat growers are aimed at conserving fuel and water and preserving the health of the soil.

½ cup butter

1 thumb-size knob of ginger, peeled and finely grated

¾ cup white sugar

⅛ tsp salt

1 tsp vanilla

6 to 8 firm pears, quartered and cored (not peeled), reserved in acidulated water (see p. 132)

½ recipe Great Pie Crust (see p. 89), chilled

Melt butter in a 10-inch oven-proof sauté pan over medium-low. Add ginger and cook until fragrant, about 1 minute, stirring often. Add sugar, salt and vanilla; stir gently until sugar is melted. Without stirring, let the mixture cook until it turns a rich caramel color. Remove from heat.

Starting at the outer edge of the pan, lay the pear halves on their sides in the pan, packing them as close together as possible to form concentric circles.

Return the pan to the stove over medium heat and cook until the pears begin to release their juices, 3 to 5 minutes. Cook until the pears are just tender and caramelized on the bottom edge, about 10 minutes. Flip each pear quarter and cook the other side until caramelized, another 10 to 15 minutes. Remove from heat and let cool in the pan to room temperature. If there's more than about ½ inch of liquid in the pan, carefully pour off and reserve the excess.

Preheat oven to 375° F. Roll out the chilled pie dough into an 11-inch round. Use the rolling pin to transfer it to the pan, and drape the dough over the pears. Fold and tuck the edge of the dough under to make a rim. Place the pan on a baking sheet and bake until crust is crisp and golden brown, about 25 minutes.

Let cool 15 minutes. Carefully pour off and reserve the pan juices with the juices reserved earlier, if any. If the reserved juices are thin, simmer over medium-low heat until thick enough to coat the back of a spoon.

Invert a large plate over the pan and quickly flip the pan and the plate over, then lift off the pan. Serve warm or at room temperature with vanilla ice cream; drizzle the caramelized juices over top. Leftovers, if you have any, won't keep more than a day or so and shouldn't be refrigerated.

# Caramel-dipped Apples

## Serves 8

This recipe is inspired by summer memories of the Puyallup Fair. Next to sounding out geoduck, pronouncing the town of Puyallup is the easiest way to determine if someone is a tourist. If they say "Poo-ya-lup," they're 100 percent tourist. Say it like a local and say "Pew-aa-lup." Late in the summer, tourists and locals alike flock to the fair. Their motivation? Winning large stuffed animals at Whac-a-Mole? Riding the vertigo-inducing, stomach-churning rides? Possibly. But we like going to the fair for an annual gustatory experience best reserved for, well, once a year. Caramel-dipped apples are a necessary part of this experience (but then so are elephant ears, curly fries and the unfortunately named "crusty pup," which is essentially a corn dog). Take yourself to your local farmers' market, locate a nice, big, juicy, tart Granny Smith, cloak it homemade caramel and think back to the end of summer "doing the Puyallup."

1 lb dark brown sugar

¾ cup unsalted butter, room temperature

1 x 10 oz can sweetened condensed milk

⅔ cup light corn syrup

¼ tsp sea salt

1 tsp vanilla

¼ cup heavy cream (32 percent)

8 apples, such as Macintosh or Granny Smith, stems removed, washed and dried

8 wooden sticks such as craft sticks, popsicle sticks or even chopsticks

Combine brown sugar, butter, condensed milk, corn syrup and salt in a heavy-bottomed pot over medium-low and stir slowly but continually to dissolve sugar until it reaches a temperature between 234° F and 240° F on a candy thermometer, or the soft-ball stage (see opposite). Remove from heat, stir in vanilla and cream and pour into a clean metal bowl. Cool until caramel is 200° F, about 15 minutes.

While caramel is cooling, line a baking sheet with buttered parchment paper and push a stick into the stem end of each apple. Dip apples in caramel and let excess caramel drip off before setting on the greased paper. Cool before eating. Chill any uneaten apples, wrapped in cellophane, up to 1 week.

**Tip**

If your apples are quite waxy, dip them in boiling water for 30 seconds to remove the wax, and dry very well.

**Tip**

Once the caramel apples have set, dip them into melted chocolate for an extra decadent Halloween treat. You can also roll them in chopped nuts, candy sprinkles or crushed candy bars!

**Tip**
The soft-ball stage is a candy test where you drop a little syrup in cold water, and as the syrup cools, it forms a soft ball that flattens when it is removed from the water.

# Olympia Oysters on the Half Shell with Apple and Tobiko Vinaigrette

### Serves 8 to 12

Aphrodite sprang from the ocean naked atop an oyster shell, and thus our favorite aphrodisiac was born. Oysters have been cultivated for more than 2000 years, and the Romans apparently fattened up their oysters with wine and pastries. Olympia oysters are the only oysters native to the Puget Sound, and they were an important food source for Washington's Native Americans. They were heavily depleted in the 1950s owing to water pollution and over-harvesting, and there has been a widespread effort (especially in the Hood Canal) to bring back the Olympias ("olys") to their previous heyday status. Olympias are the smallest species of oyster, measuring in at a Lilliputian 2½ inches in diameter. Don't, however, let their small size belie their power; they can filter about 9 to 12 gallons of water a day—making them an important ecological helper.

**pinch of unbleached sugar**

**juice from 1 lemon**

**½ tsp freshly ground pepper**

**¼ cup finely diced green apple**

**¼ cup finely chopped chives**

**1 x 1 oz jar of tobiko (flying fish caviar; see below)**

**1 x 1 oz jar of black lumpfish caviar**

**24 Olympia oysters in the shell**

**crushed ice**

**2 lemons, cut into wedges**

To make vinaigrette, in a small bowl, mix together the first 5 ingredients plus 1 Tbsp of each caviar, reserving remainder, and set aside.

Shuck oysters, leaving each one in cupped half of its shell. Arrange oyster half-shells on a platter of crushed ice, and nestle remaining caviar in the center. Put a teaspoon of the vinaigrette on each oyster. Decorate platter with lemon wedges. Serve with remaining vinaigrette, making sure that the oysters are kept cool.

### Tip

Oysters should be purchased alive and fresh from a reputable source, preferably a store specializing in seafood. The shell should be tightly closed, or, if the shell is slightly open, it should close promptly when tapped. If the shell is open and does not close when tapped, or if the shell is broken, throw the oyster out. Oysters should be stored on ice and covered with a damp cloth in the refrigerater, to allow them to breathe.

*Tobiko caviar is an inexpensive fish roe that you have probably tried if you eat sushi. It is available in a range of colors, from pale yellow to red, and flavors, such as wasabi. It has a nice pop when you eat it. You can purchase it from a fresh fish market, Japanese specialty food stores or order it on-line.*

It is still widely believed that oysters are only safe to eat during months that have an "r" in their name. It is believed that this myth came about when poor refrigeration led to spoilage during months with no "r." Another reason is that European oysters (Ostrea edulis) aren't desirable during non-r months. These oysters are unique in that baby oysters are held by the mother oyster until shells develop (and they are therefore inedible during the summer). American oysters, on the other hand, are actually at their peak in May and June as they begin to store gylcogen and animal starch in preparation for spawning (making them fatter and tastier).

# Grilled Asian Pear and Avocado Salad with Garam Masala Vinaigrette

**Serves 4**

At one time, Asian or Indian food ingredients were only available in specialty ethnic markets. Now, with the rising popularity of ethnic cuisine and the proliferation of multi-ethnic communities in Washington, these ingredients are now available in local grocery stores throughout the state. This recipe combines both Asian and Indian flavors to create a mouth-watering salad using the fresh citrus note of lemongrass and the heady aroma of garam masala. Finding fresh garam masala (typically a blend of coriander, cinnamon, cumin, cloves and black pepper) makes the world of difference in this recipe. Making your own at home easily solves that problem, and isn't too hard. For a large selection of Asian pears, look for Rockridge Orchards bounty in western Washington farmers' markets. They grow 3200 Asian pear trees spanning 17 different varieties. The other secret to this recipe is the grilled avocado—once you have tried it, you'll never eat an ungrilled avocado again.

¼ cup canola oil

2 Tbsp honey

2 Asian pears, halved

2 avocados, peeled, halved and cut into 4 slices

½ lb baby salad greens

sea salt and freshly ground pepper

**Garam Masala Vinaigrette**

3 Tbsp garam masala (see opposite)

1 Tbsp plus ¼ cup olive oil

1 Tbsp rice wine vinegar

1-inch piece from the thick end of a lemongrass stalk, minced

Mix oil and honey together in a small bowl. Brush on Asian pears and avocados and grill over medium heat for about 5 minutes. Season with salt and pepper.

For the vinaigrette, mix the garam masala into 1 Tbsp of oil to form a paste. Then whisk garam masala paste, oil, rice wine vinegar and lemongrass together in a small bowl. Add the vinaigrette to the salad greens and serve on individual plates with the pears and avocados.

**Garam Masala**
**Makes about ½ cup**

Combine everything but nutmeg in a dry heavy skillet over medium-high heat. Toast the spices, stirring occasionally, until they are fragrant and several shades darker, about 10 minutes. Set aside to cool.

Transfer the mixture to a spice mill, coffee grinder or mortar, and grind to a powder. Stir in nutmeg. Use immediately or store up to 3 months in an airtight container in a cool, dry place.

3-inch stick of cinnamon, broken up

2 Tbsp black peppercorns

2 Tbsp cardamom seeds

2 Tbsp coriander seeds

2 Tbsp cumin seeds

1 tsp whole cloves

1 tsp grated nutmeg

# Ozette Potato and Roasted Garlic Chowder

**Serves 4**

A true local treasure, the Ozette potato (an heirloom fingerling) was brought by the Spanish to Neah Bay from South America in 1791. The Makah tribe cultivated it for the next 200 years. Knobby, thin-skinned, earthy and deeply satisfying as only a potato can be, Ozettes have been recognized by Slow Food as a special heritage food of the Northwest. Washington's Full Circle Farm (Carnation), Nature's Last Stand (Carnation) and Half Moon Acre Farm (Vashon) are growing our dearly beloved Ozette. Roasting neutralizes the pungency of the garlic and brings out its sweetness. Stop by your closest winter farmers' market and find some local garlic (large bulbs are perfect for roasting). Delicious and nutritious, this soup is sure to ward off the usual wintertime ailments.

**2 medium onions, diced**

**¼ cup unsalted butter**

**1 Tbsp olive oil**

**2 cups diced celery**

**1 cup diced carrots**

**12 Ozette potatoes, peeled and diced**

**1 bay leaf**

**vegetable or chicken stock, enough to just cover vegetables**

**2 bulbs roasted garlic (see opposite), cloves squeezed out and roughly chopped**

**2 cups heavy cream (32 percent)**

**sea salt and freshly ground pepper to taste**

**¼ cup chopped fresh herbs such as parsley, thyme or mint**

In a heavy pot, sauté the onions in the butter and oil until they turn golden. Add the vegetables and bay leaf and cover with stock. Simmer for 15 minutes. Add the roasted garlic and cream, and simmer for 10 to 15 minutes more or until the potatoes are cooked and the soup is reduced and creamy. Season to taste with salt and pepper. Ladle soup into bowls and garnish with a sprinkle of herbs.

**Roasted Garlic**
You can roast as little or as much garlic as you want. We
tend to roast 5 or 6 bulbs at a time so we will have leftovers
to last a week. Preheat the oven to 350° F. Slice the top of
each bulb of garlic to expose the cloves, and lay them cut
side up in a baking dish. Drizzle with olive oil and sprinkle
with salt. Roast 20 to 30 minutes or until cloves are tender.
Remove from oven and set aside until cool enough to han-
dle. The buttery flesh of the cloves will come out of the bulb
easily when you squeeze it (throw out the papery skin of the
bulb). Alternatively, you can serve the whole roasted bulbs
as a garnish for grilled meats or vegetables.

# Hale's Cream Ale and Washington Cougar Gold Cheddar Soup

## Serves 4

Twenty-five years ago, the Pacific Northwest was a vast wasteland of beer options. Local, micro-brewed beers and brewpubs in the 1970s in Washington were but a distant twinkle in some baby boomer's eye. Those were the days when Bud was considered a premium beer. Luckily for beer afficionados, the beer industry has exploded in this region. It was destined to happen, for what a waste it would be if all those local hops couldn't be put to good use (most of the world's hops are grown right here in the Yakima Valley). Hale's, founded in the early days of 1983, produces a variety of popular English-style ales. For this recipe, we've picked the smooth as silk Hale's Cream Ale (brewed from pale malted barley, crystal and wheat malts, Centennial, Nugget and Cascade hops, Hale's special yeast and filtered water). A truly local combination pairs Hale's Cream Ale with Washington State University's Cougar Gold Cheese. A white Cheddar packaged in now-iconic 30-oz tin cans, Cougar Gold received a gold medal at the 2006 World Cheese Awards.

2 medium onions, diced

1 Tbsp olive oil

¼ cup unsalted butter

2 cups diced celery

1 cup diced parsnips

4 medium potatoes, peeled and diced

1 bay leaf

vegetable or chicken stock, enough to just cover vegetables

2 cups heavy cream (32 percent)

2 cups grated sharp Washington Cougar Gold Cheddar

½ to 1 bottle of Hale's Cream Ale, about 6 to 12 oz or to taste

sea salt and freshly ground pepper

In a heavy pot, sauté onions in butter and oil until they turn golden. Add celery, parsnips, potatoes, bay leaf and enough stock to cover everything. Simmer for 15 minutes, then add the cream and simmer for 10 to 15 minutes more or until the potatoes are cooked and the soup is reduced and creamy. Remove soup from heat and blend in cheese in small batches. Purée soup in a blender and return to medium-low heat and stir in ale to taste. Season with salt and pepper and serve heated in bowls. If you like, garnish with Parley Oil (see p. 103).

*The Washington State University Creamery produces 250,000 cans of cheese each year—80 percent is the fantastic Cougar Gold. This cheese is aged at least a year and is claimed to last indefinitely in the refrigerator in an unopened can.*

# Cioppino with Fennel and Saffron

## Serves 6

"That small gift that looked like a mere taste in a simple thick-lipped bowl, but that caught my breath as I brought it near my mouth, caught me with this aroma, this complex, maritime hint of something ancient..." said Seattle editor and songwriter Leslie Eliel on tasting cioppino at Brad's Swingside Cafe. No sweeter words have been spoken on one of our country's favorite stews. Cioppino comes to us originally from Italy, and it entered our collective consciousness when it took root in the San Francisco Bay area. It was there that Italian immigrants from Genoa replaced traditional Genoese ingredients with the fresh fish available to them on the West Coast. Refreshed with a distinctly local flair, Seattle-style cioppino almost always has a mixture of Dungeness crab, shrimp, clams, scallops, mussels and Pacific snapper (rockfish).

**2 lbs Pacific Snapper fillet**

**1 lb fresh shrimp, tails on**

**½ lb each clams, mussels and scallops**

**1 crab, cooked, cleaned and cracked**

**2 Tbsp extra virgin olive oil**

**1 small onion, minced**

**1 medium fennel bulb, diced**

**1 cup white wine**

**3 cloves garlic, minced**

**zest from ½ orange, minced**

**pinch of saffron, or to taste, dissolved in ¼ cup warm stock**

**4 cups tomato sauce**

**3 cups fish stock**

**sea salt and freshly ground pepper**

**½ cup fresh basil for garnish**

Wash all fish and seafood, except crab, and pat dry. In a heavy-bottomed pot, heat oil and sauté onion. Stir in fennel and sauté for 5 minutes. Add wine and garlic, and simmer for 10 minutes. Stir in orange zest, saffron, tomato sauce and stock, and simmer for 10 minutes. Nestle fish fillets and seafood into the sauce, making sure to cover them with liquid. Cover, bring back to a simmer over medium-high heat and cook until clams and mussels open, about 10 to 12 minutes. Season with salt and pepper. Serve hot in warmed bowls, garnished with fresh basil.

### Tip

It is traditional to serve cioppino with polenta and a bottle of Chianti. If you have trouble finding polenta and mascarpone, try an Italian deli.

### Polenta with Mascarpone

Bring milk and cream to a boil. Whisk in polenta and cook, stirring continuously, for 20 minutes. Season to taste with salt and pepper. Serve hot topped with mascarpone. You can also pour polenta into a 9 x 12-inch rectangular baking dish. Once cooled, it can be sliced and pan-grilled with butter.

**4 cups milk**

**½ cup heavy cream (32 percent)**

**1 cup polenta**

**salt and pepper to taste**

**1 cup mascarpone**

# Caramelized Onion and Goat Cheese Tart

## Serves 6

While many goat cheese producers keep their goats producing milk year-round, Jumpin' Good Goat Dairy in Ocean Park prefers to follow the natural cycle of the goat. They breed their goats in September and milk through October. They let the does go "dry" for the final three months of their pregnancy and cease cheese production for those months (November, December and January). Milk production ramps back up again in February when the kids are born. Aged cheeses are available through the dry months to tide loyal customers over. Also be sure to watch for delicious goat cheeses from Monteillet in Walla Walla and Mt. Townsend in Port Townsend.

**1 Tbsp oil**

**1 Tbsp butter**

**6 medium yellow onions, thinly sliced**

**sea salt to taste**

**1 tsp sugar**

**1 Tbsp balsamic vinegar**

**Béchamel**

**2 Tbsp butter**

**2 Tbsp flour**

**1 cup milk**

**1 bay leaf**

**pinch of nutmeg**

**1 x ¾ lb package of frozen puff pastry, thawed**

**egg wash made with 1 beaten egg and a splash of water**

**8 oz goat cheese**

**2 Tbsp chopped fresh herbs, such as parsley, thyme or sage (optional)**

Place oil and butter in a large pan over medium heat. Add the onions, season with salt and cook until softened, about 6 minutes. Stir in the sugar and balsamic vinegar, turn the heat to medium-low and cook for 30 to 45 minutes, stirring often, until nicely caramelized.

To make the béchamel, melt the butter in a small, heavy saucepan over low heat. Add flour into melted butter and stir for 5 to 7 minutes. Slowly add milk, then the bay leaf and nutmeg, stirring constantly, and cook for about 10 more minutes until smooth and thick.

Preheat oven to 400° F. Roll out the pastry to ⅛ inch thick and place on a rectangular baking sheet. Prick all over with a fork. Brush the outside edges, about ½ inch, with egg wash.

Combine onions and béchamel sauce in a medium bowl. Crumble in goat cheese (and fresh herbs, if desired), and stir to combine.

Spread onion mixture onto pastry and bake for 15 to 20 minutes until pastry is puffed and golden. Let sit 10 minutes before cutting into squares. Serve warm or at room temperature with a lightly dressed green salad and Port Sauce (see opposite).

**Port Sauce**

In a small saucepan, combine Port and stock and reduce over medium heat until thick and syrupy.

**1 cup Port wine**

**½ cup chicken stock**

**Tip**

This tart is perfect for picnics, potlucks and lazy Sunday brunches. Best served at room temperature or slightly warm, it makes a great "do ahead" choice for traveling or entertaining. It also could be cooked in individual tart shells for easy serving.

# Braised Kale Crostini with Raisins, Olives and Aged Pecorino Romano

### Serves 6 as an appetizer

It would be safe to say that delicious, nutritious kale is one of the most reliable year-round crops in these parts. Sadly, many people think they don't like the crinkly leaves, which are often used as garnish and not as the star of the plate. This recipe will turn around your most fervent nose-wrinkling dissenter. Braised just long enough to make the leaves tender and imbued with a touch of brown sugar and balsamic vinegar, these crostini have an addictive savory-sweet-sour quality that is played off perfectly with a paper-thin slice of Pecorino Romano from Black Sheep Creamery, aged for one year at a 100-year old farm just six miles from Chehalis.

**2 bunches of kale (dinosaur kale, or lacinato, is our favorite)**

**2 Tbsp extra-virgin olive oil, and more to drizzle over top**

**1 shallot, minced**

**pinch of salt**

**3 large cloves garlic, minced**

**pinch of red chile flakes**

**2 tsp balsamic vinegar**

**½ cup pitted, chopped Kalamata olives**

**¼ cup golden raisins**

**1 tsp brown sugar**

**chicken broth or water, as needed**

**sea salt and freshly ground pepper to taste**

**¼ cup toasted pine nuts (see p. 134)**

**6 slices of artisan bread (such as Essential's Columbia)**

**aged Pecorino Romano, shaved for garnish**

Strip the kale leaves away from the thick stem and discard the stems. Wash leaves well to remove all grit. Shake water from them but don't worry about drying them well. Slice into long, thin (about ½-inch) strips. Heat oil in a large saucepan over medium-high. Sauté shallot until soft. Add a pinch of salt, then the garlic and chile flakes. Mix well and cook for another minute.

Increase heat to high. Add greens with the water still clinging to them. Add vinegar, olives, raisins, brown sugar and a few tablespoons of chicken broth or water. Stir, cover and let greens cook down for 5 minutes. Stir, add more liquid if greens are dry, cover and cook for 5 to 10 more minutes.

Add salt and pepper to taste, and toss in the pine nuts. Taste again. Greens should be tender and a little bit sweet and sour. Toast the bread and then pile some greens on top. Garnish with cheese and drizzle with olive oil.

**Tip**
This recipe also makes a delicious
light meal when served with a
poached egg on top.

# White Wine and Garlic Mussels

**Serves 4 to 6**

8 NW Front St., Coupeville, is home to Toby's Tavern, where a beer at the bar, a try at pull tabs and a friendly chat with the bartender all occur through the steamy haze of a big, fat bowl of garlic-laced mussels. No need to ponder the 100-mile diet concept here because your dinner was harvested around the corner at Penn Cove Shellfish. Your biggest decision is not figuring out whether they are the best mussels you ever had, but whether you should get the small bowl or the large bowl. Over at Taylor Shellfish Farms (various locations) they cultivate Mediterranean mussels ("Meds"). Meds are in season in the summer when the local cultivated mussels (Puget Sound blue and North Atlantic blue) are spawning. All this is to say that mussel fans have a year-round supply of their favorite bivalve. Meds were first located along the Strait of Juan de Fuca, around 1989 (but they may have been in the Puget Sound long before... rumored to have come over as stowaways on boats from Europe). Where the local mussels are considered slightly more briny, meds are fatter and a bit sweeter.

**4 lbs mussels**

**1 cup white wine, such as Chardonnay**

Scrub mussels under cool running water and remove any beards. Discard mussels that don't close when gently tapped.

**4 cloves garlic, minced**

**1 Tbsp butter**

**¼ cup chopped chives**

Place white wine and garlic in a large pot with a lid and bring to a boil. Add mussels to the pot, cover and reduce heat, cooking for about 5 to 6 minutes. Discard any mussels that have not opened. With a slotted spoon, transfer the mussels into serving dishes.

Turn heat to high and bring the remaining liquid to a boil. Cook for 2 to 3 minutes until it has reduced slightly, and whisk in butter. Spoon the sauce over mussels, sprinkle with chives and serve hot.

### Tip
Use fresh mussels within 24 hours of purchasing them. The best way to store fresh mussels is to put them in a colander and place the colander into a bowl. Cover the mussels with ice and then with a damp towel. The mussels will stay very cold and have good air circulation, without being submerged (or drowned) in water.

*Mussels are at their highest quality in the 6 months leading up to their spawning period and, conversely, at their poorest quality during and just after spawning.*

# Wild Black Cod and Lentils with Vinaigrette

### Serves 4

Black cod is one of the hottest items on many of Washington's top restaurant menus and—in our humble opinion—for good reason. Black cod, also known as sablefish or butterfish, is high in healthy omega-3 fatty acids; and its flesh is so unctuous, so divinely rich, that salmon can seem downright lean in comparison. Black cod is caught in the deep waters off Alaska and on down the coast. Traditionally, most black cod has been exported to Japan and Hong Kong, but it is now commonly available at many fishmongers around the state and for that we are very, very thankful.

**4 black cod fillets, about 4 oz each**

**sea salt and freshly ground pepper**

**splash of olive oil**

**1 cup cooked red lentils (see Tip)**

**Vinaigrette**

**¼ cup olive oil**

**¼ cup lemon juice**

**1 Tbsp chopped fresh thyme**

**1 Tbsp chopped fresh chives**

**1 Tbsp orange zest**

**sea salt and freshly ground pepper**

**½ lb mixed salad greens with fresh herbs**

Season black cod with salt and pepper. Heat a grill pan over medium-high and add a splash of oil. Sear fish, about 2 to 3 minutes per side. Remove from heat and set aside.

Mix together warmed, cooked lentils in a bowl with olive oil, lemon juice, thyme, chives, orange zest, salt and pepper.

Serve grilled fish on a bed of lentils and mixed salad with fresh herbs.

**Tip**
To cook lentils, pour 1 cup of cleaned, dry lentils into 3 cups salted, boiling water. Reduce heat and simmer until the lentils are *al dente*, about 20 minutes. One cup of dry lentils makes 2 to 2½ cups cooked lentils.

# Gravlax

## Serves 6

In a typical Swedish smorgasbord (self-serve buffet) you will find a number of cold fish dishes, such as pickled herring, lutefisk (cod or Pollock marinated in potash lye) and gravlax. This last dish is centuries old, and its name means "buried salmon"—Swedes used to preserve salmon by burying it in pits and letting it ferment over a period of about six months, sometimes longer. Traditional gravlax, made only with salmon, salt, sugar and fresh dill, is a great way to showcase the flavor of the salmon; if desired, the recipe below can be made with the other ingredients omitted. If you want a Washington-style Scandinavian experience, pack your gravlax and some crackers and other vittles and take a walking tour of the Ballard neighborhood in Seattle. Ballard has deep Scandinavian roots—in 1880 there were only 190 Scandinavians in all of King County, and between 1890 and 1910, close to 150,000 more settled in our region, many going to Ballard to work on the railroad, in the mills or on the waterfront. Today, young hipsters go to Copper Gate, a bar that pays homage to its roots. On the menu: meatballs and gravlax to be downed with shots of Aquavit or a lingonberry soda.

1 Tbsp peppercorns

1 Tbsp coriander seeds

1 large bunch of fresh dill, washed and spun dry

2 lbs fresh wild salmon fillet (skin on, scaled)

⅓ cup salt

⅓ cup unbleached sugar

2 Tbsp Aquavit

fresh salsa for garnish (optional)

Toast peppercorns and coriander seeds in a small skillet over medium heat until they start to jump in the pan. Remove and crush with mortar and pestle. Lay out a piece of parchment paper and put ⅓ of the fresh dill, whole, in middle. Prick skin side of salmon in 6 places with a sharp knife and lay skin side down on dill. Mix salt, sugar, pepper and coriander and sprinkle evenly over salmon flesh. Sprinkle Aquavit over spices and lay remaining dill overtop.

Wrap parchment around fillet and then enclose in plastic wrap. Place skin side down in a glass baking dish, set another dish on top and weigh down with 2 or 3 soup cans. Let marinate in fridge for 48 hours.

When ready to serve, remove fish from wrap and gently wipe clean. Slice paper-thin and serve with your favorite accompaniments, such as dark rye bread, horseradish, dill cream cheese and pickles. To serve gravlax as an appetizer, lay slices out in a single layer to cover the bottom of a plate. Garnish each serving with salsa, if desired.

**Tip**
Store extra gravlax unsliced in the refrigerator, brushed with olive oil to keep it from drying out.

*Aquavit, or "water of life," is a Scandinavian liquor similar to vodka, distilled from potato or grain mash and infused with herbs and spices. It is believed to possess medicinal properties and to aid in the digestion of food, which is why it is an important beverage during festive occasions.*

# Blackened Trout with Oven-dried Tomatoes

**Serves 2**

A favorite pastime for many Washington residents during the warm months of the year is to head out to fish on one of the many lakes that dot the region. Nothing tastes better than a breakfast of pan-fried trout with brown butter and some eggs cooked over an open fire. However, for those winter evenings when you are in the comfort of your own home, many local fishmongers sell excellent farm-raised trout that will bring back those summer memories. The blackening spices in this recipe will warm you up and the oven-dried tomatoes are a hearty version of the sweet, vine-ripened summer variety.

**2 lbs Roma tomatoes, halved lengthwise**

**3 cloves garlic, minced**

**¼ cup chopped fresh thyme**

**sea salt and freshly ground pepper to taste**

**½ cup extra virgin olive oil**

**Spice Mixture**
**2 tsp paprika**

**2 tsp chipotle powder or chili powder**

**2 tsp ground cumin**

**2 tsp dried thyme**

**1 tsp each sea salt and freshly ground pepper**

**2 fresh trout, gutted but whole**

**2 Tbsp canola oil**

Preheat oven to 250° F. Scoop out seeds from the tomatoes. Mix the garlic with the thyme, salt and pepper and olive oil. Place the tomatoes cut side up in a roasting pan and drizzle with the garlic mixture. Bake for at least 3 hours or until the tomatoes are dehydrated but still chewy.

Mix all the spices together in a bowl. Rinse trout with water and pat dry with paper towels. Brush oil on the trout and rub it all over with the spice mixture.

Heat oil in a heavy-bottomed skillet until it is smoking hot. Place the prepared trout in the skillet. Cook for 2 to 4 minutes and turn over. Cook until the fish is firm and cooked through, 3 to 4 minutes. To test doneness, the fish should flake easily with a fork but should not be dry. Serve with oven-dried tomatoes on the side.

**Tip**
Oven-drying tomatoes is a great way to preserve these tasty bits of summer sunshine. Grow tomatoes in your garden or in containers, or pick them up at farmers' markets. Any leftover tomatoes can be covered in olive oil and stored in a jar. They will keep for up to 3 weeks refrigerated.

# Hazelnut-roasted Pork with Pear Cider

### Serves 8 to 10

Now is one of the most exciting times to be a fan of farm fresh-food in general, and locally and humanely raised meats in particular. There are many options to choose from when looking for pork in Washington state. Chefs in the know get in line for one of Mark Baker's pigs (he only raises 10 to 20 a year in Gig Harbor). For a steadier supply, stop by one of the eight PCC Natural Markets in the greater Seattle area and look for the Northwest Heritage Pork label. It comes from Pure Country Pork Farms in Ephreta, where farmer Paul Klingeman raises about 8000 pigs a year. Pure Country is the first pig farm in Washington to receive the highly coveted Food Alliance certification.

### Stuffing

2 Tbsp olive oil

1 onion, finely chopped

4 cloves garlic, roughly chopped

¼ cup chopped fresh rosemary

¼ cup chopped fresh thyme

2 cups roughly chopped hazelnuts

¼ cup chicken stock

2 Tbsp dry breadcrumbs

1 Tbsp dark brown sugar

3 lb pork loin rib roast, patted dry, room temperature

sea salt and freshly ground pepper

butcher's twine

3 to 6 sprigs of fresh rosemary

1 Tbsp olive oil

### Glaze

¾ cup pear cider

¼ cup chicken broth

3 Tbsp honey

Preheat oven to 400° F. Heat oil in a pan and cook onions, garlic, rosemary and thyme for a few minutes. Add hazelnuts. Stir in chicken stock, breadcrumbs and brown sugar, and set stuffing aside.

Turn the roast fat side down. Slit lengthwise, almost but not quite all the way through, to form a long pocket, leaving a ½-inch border of uncut meat at each end. Sprinkle generously with salt and pepper. Fill the cavity with the stuffing. Tie loin together with butcher's twine or heavy-duty kitchen string at 1½-inch intervals. Slide the rosemary sprigs under the twine. Brush with remaining olive oil and sprinkle generously with salt and pepper. Set fat side up, diagonally or curved (so it fits), on a large baking sheet or jelly-roll pan.

Mix cider, chicken broth and honey together. Brush glaze mixture on meat.

Roast in the oven until a meat thermometer registers 150° to 155° F, about 2 hours, occasionally brushing with the pan drippings. Let roast rest 15 to 20 minutes out of the oven while you make the Port Sauce (see opposite), then transfer to a carving board. Slice pork roast and serve with sauce.

### Port Sauce

Stir juices around pan to loosen browned bits. Pour through a strainer into a small pan, and stir in Port and chicken stock. Bring to simmer and cook until lightly thickened.

**¼ cup Port wine**
**¼ cup chicken stock**

*Food Alliance is one of the most comprehensive agricultural certification bodies today. It ensures that successful applicants go well beyond other animal welfare certification programs. Applicants apply for certification based on the entire health of their farm (safe and fair working conditions, humane treatment of the animals, no use of hormones or antibiotics, no genetically modified organisms, commitment to soil and water conservation and wildlife habitat preservation, among other things).*

# Broccoli and Tempeh Rice Bowl

**Serves 4**

Washington state, and more specifically Seattle, is one of the healthiest places in the U.S. We truly value exercise and healthy eating here (when not slugging wine, beer and coffee). This dish combines one of our favorite green vegetables with tempeh, a soybean product very important in vegetarian diets. Tempeh originated in Indonesia and is made in a slightly different way from tofu. Tofu is made by heating and coagulating soy milk (similar to how cheese is made), and tempeh is made by cooking and fermenting whole soybeans. Tempeh has a stronger flavor, firmer texture and higher content of protein, dietary fiber and vitamins than tofu. You can find tempeh at many local health food stores or even major grocery stores such as Whole Foods or Metropolitan Market. Tempeh's firm texture makes it a great substitute for meat in many recipes.

2 Tbsp soy sauce

1 Tbsp mirin or sweet rice wine

2 Tbsp light miso

1 tsp toasted sesame oil

¼ tsp cornstarch

2 tsp grape seed or canola oil

1 Tbsp finely chopped ginger

2 tsp chopped lemongrass, tender bottom part only

2 cloves garlic, minced

1 package of Indonesian-style tempeh, cut into ¼-inch strips

1 head of broccoli, cut into florets

¼ cup each sliced yellow and red pepper

¼ cup snow peas

¼ cup green onions, cut in ¼-inch diagonal strips

2 tsp black sesame seeds

¼ tsp sea salt

2 cups hot, cooked brown rice

In a small bowl, combine soy sauce, mirin, miso, sesame oil and cornstarch. Stir with a whisk and set aside. Heat oil in a large skillet over medium-high and sauté ginger, lemongrass and garlic for 1 minute or just until mixture begins to brown. Add tempeh and sauté for 2 minutes, and add broccoli, peppers and snow peas and sauté for 1 minute. Add reserved mixture to skillet and cook for 1 minute, until sauce has slightly thickened. Remove from heat and stir in green onions, sesame seeds and salt. Serve over rice.

**Tip**
Soak your broccoli in warm, salted water to get rid of any critters. As with all members of the cabbage family, broccoli is best used within a few days of picking to retain its sweet flavor and mild odor.

# Tempura

## Serves 6 to 8

Batter-laced deep-frying is a method of cooking that was introduced to Japan by Portuguese missionaries during the 16th century. By the 17th century, Tokyo street vendors were selling tempura, using fish freshly caught in Tokyo Bay and most often fried in sesame oil. This traditional cooking method has caught on in Washington owing to the huge interest in Japanese cuisine. Tempura—when done well—can be an exceptionally light and delicate dish, confounding those expecting fried food to be heavy and greasy. Tempura is so popular in Seattle that we even have a Seattle Tempura Roll, where salmon and asparagus are tucked into a sushi roll that is then dipped in tempura batter and fried. Be sure to choose the freshest possible ingredients, such as spot prawns, salmon, local summer squash and even zucchini blossoms.

peanut oil (see Tip)

1 egg, beaten

1 cup cold beer

2 Tbsp dry white wine

½ cup flour

¼ cup rice flour

¼ cup corn starch

variety of vegetables and seafood, cut into bite-sized pieces

Heat peanut oil in a pan or deep fryer until temperature is 375° F. Combine egg, beer and white wine in a small bowl. In another bowl, combine flour, rice flour and cornstarch. Add liquid to dry mixture and very lightly mix together. The batter should look lumpy. Dip vegetables and seafood in tempura batter and fry in small batches until golden and crispy.

**Tip**

For deep-frying, peanut oil should be 2 to 3 inches deep. If you have a deep fryer, follow the manufacturer's directions.

**Tip**

Keys to tasty, crispy tempura are a very light mixing of the batter—lumps are GOOD—and using an ice-cold liquid, preferably one that is carbonated. To avoid greasy, soggy tempura, it is important to maintain the proper temperature of the oil, so it's best to have a thermometer on hand.

The word tempura comes from the Latin ad tempora cuaresmae, *meaning* "in the time of Lent." As good Catholics, the Portuguese missionaries substituted fish for meat at this time of the year, and batter-frying *was a* popular presentation.

# Pappardelle with Black Winter Truffles

### Serves 4

Many of Washington's top regional chefs are using truffles to enhance local ingredients and dishes. Often called "the perfume of the earth itself," the truffle is a coveted aphrodisiac, strongly scented with a musky earthiness that is evocative of sex and mystery. Most truffles are harvested in late fall or winter and you can find fresh truffles at specialty markets across the state, but they will cost you a pretty penny—they run anywhere from $700 to $3000 per pound for truffles from France and Italy. If you are more budget conscious, you can more easily find truffle butter, versatile truffle oil (make sure it is made with real truffles!) or even truffle salt, giving you the pleasure of the flavor at a more reasonable cost. For local flavor, drive down to Oregon and get to know the black and white truffles being harvested there. Oregon's truffles are not quite the same as Europe's, but they're deliciously fragrant, fresher and a world more accessible in price (only $100 to $450 a pound).

### Cream Sauce

1 Tbsp butter

¼ cup finely chopped onion

½ cup white wine

½ cup heavy cream (32 percent)

sea salt and freshly ground pepper

¼ cup grated Parmesan cheese

1 lb fresh pappardelle, homemade (see opposite) or store-bought

1 medium black winter truffle, grated, sliced or shaved

Melt butter in a skillet and sauté onion until soft. Add white wine and simmer until half the liquid is reduced. Stir in cream and simmer for 5 minutes. Season with salt and pepper.

Bring a large pot of salted water to a boil, add the pappardelle and cook until *al dente*, for about 5 minutes. Drain and transfer pasta to the skillet with the cream sauce and add Parmesan cheese. Toss gently to mix and transfer to a warm serving bowl. Grate fresh truffle over pasta and serve.

### Tip

Have a pot of boiling water ready first, and you can prepare the sauce and cook the pasta at the same time.

**Homemade Pasta**

Mix flour and eggs on low speed in a
heavy-duty electric mixer until mixture has
a coarse, crumbly look, like corn meal. Add
water in small quantities until the mixture
starts to hold together. Switch to the
dough hook on the mixer, or knead by hand
7 to 10 minutes. Dough should not be sticky or in separate pieces. Add
a little more liquid if needed, or a little more flour if sticky. Cover with
plastic wrap and let dough rest 15 to 30 minutes. Roll through a pasta
machine according to the manufacturer's instructions.

To cook, make sure water is at a full boil and very
well salted. Fresh pasta cooks very quickly and
will rise to the top of the water when done.
Drain in a colander and do not rinse.

1½ cups semolina flour

2 eggs

2 to 3 tsp lukewarm water

# Balsamic-glazed Root Vegetables

## Serves 4

The term "root vegetable" is used to describe all vegetables grown underground, including potatoes, carrots, onions, rutabagas and beets. Before greenhouses and imported fruits and vegetables, root vegetables were important winter food because they were easy to grow, lasted months in the cellar and were carbohydrate-dense and very filling. Today in Washington, many of the state's top chefs, who are committed to putting local produce on their tables, are finding new and creative ways to incorporate our great winter crops into their menus. This recipe uses the sweetness of reduced balsamic vinegar to enhance the earthy flavors of these winter staples.

### Root Vegetables

1 lb baby potatoes, a variety if possible, washed and halved or quartered, depending on size

2 medium parsnips, peeled and quartered lengthwise, then halved

1 medium yam, halved then sliced ¼-inch thick

1 small beet, washed and quartered with skin on

1 large carrot, peeled and quartered lengthwise, then halved

1 bulb garlic, broken into cloves, peeled and left whole

1 small yellow onion, peeled and quartered

chopped fresh parsley

### Marinade

¼ cup balsamic vinegar

¼ cup extra virgin olive oil or melted butter

2 Tbsp honey

¼ cup finely chopped fresh parsley

sea salt and freshly ground pepper to taste

2 sprigs of fresh thyme

2 sprigs of fresh rosemary

Preheat oven to 375° F. Combine first 4 ingredients of the marinade in a medium bowl and set aside.

Place the vegetables into a large mixing bowl. Pour the prepared marinade over top, season with salt and pepper, and toss to coat. Place into 13 x 9-inch pan and assemble the rosemary and thyme sprigs on top. Roast vegetables uncovered, turning once or twice, for about 45 minutes or until the edges are golden brown and they pierce easily with a knife. Toss with fresh parsley and serve as a side dish.

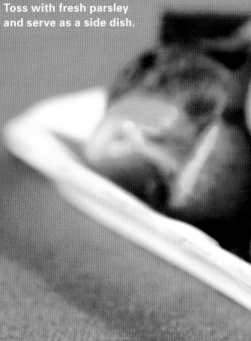

Balsamic vinegar is an aged reduction sauce that originates in the Modena region of Italy. The best balsamic vinegar is aged a long time, comes in very small bottles and is very expensive. Instead, try a cheaper variety, but not the cheapest—it's most likely red vinegar and brown sugar or caramel.

# Kabocha Squash with Wilted Mizuna and Crispy Pancetta

## Serves 6 to 8

Willie Green's Organic Farm in Monroe grows a mean bunch of mizuna. A bit spicy, mizuna is a Japanese green that is lightly mustard flavored and delicious eaten raw in salads or wilted briefly over high heat. In this recipe we have paired it with another vegetable with Japanese ties: kabocha squash. It was originally discovered in the Americas, and Columbus brought it back to Europe. It eventually reached Japan, where it took hold in the cuisine and is often used as a staple in vegetable tempura. Delightfully sweet with a chestnut-like texture, kabocha is the perfect foil for the peppery bite of mizuna and the salty meatiness of pancetta. Bring Jeff Miller, the owner of Willie Green's, a sample of this dish and thank him for his contribution!

**8 oz chopped pancetta**

**1 medium sweet onion, diced**

**1 small kabocha squash, seeded, peeled and diced into ¾-inch pieces**

**3 cloves garlic, minced**

**1 cup chicken stock**

**2 bunches of mizuna**

**sea salt and freshly ground pepper to taste**

**¼ cup grated or shaved Asiago cheese**

Cook pancetta in a large sauté pan over medium heat until crispy. Remove from the pan, drain on paper towels and set aside.

In the same pan, cook onions in the pancetta drippings over medium-low heat, stirring occasionally, until softened. Increase heat to medium and add squash. Cook, stirring occasionally, until lightly browned, about 5 minutes. Add garlic and cook until fragrant, about 1 minute. Pour in chicken stock and bring to a simmer. Cook until squash is tender and most of the liquid has evaporated, about 10 minutes. Stir in mizuna and cook until greens are tender and beginning to wilt, about 1 or 2 minutes more. Season to taste with salt and pepper. Stir in Asiago and pancetta, and serve.

# Apple Muffins with Ginger Glaze

### Makes 12

For this lazy Sunday morning recipe, we're suggesting two well-known Washington state apples. First the Jonagold, with a name that hints at its parentage (it's a cross between a Jonathan and a Golden Delicious). Jonagolds are bright red over a background of gold and are in season in September and October. Best eaten right around harvest, Jonagolds are notable for their beauty, size and sweet-tart flavor. Cameos are relatively new to Washington, having been discovered in the 1980s as a chance seedling in Dryden; they come to market pale yellow with red stripes and are known for their tart crispness. Cameos are also known for their long storage life. Look for them in mid-October.

**1 Jonagold or Cameo apple**

**2 cups flour**

**1 Tbsp baking powder**

**½ tsp cinnamon**

**¼ tsp salt**

**⅓ cup unsalted butter**

**⅓ cup packed brown sugar**

**2 large eggs**

**⅔ cup buttermilk**

**Glaze**

**⅓ cup ginger jelly**

Preheat oven to 400° F and grease a muffin pan. Core and peel apple and cut into ¼-inch chunks. Into a large bowl, sift together flour, baking powder, cinnamon and salt. In a saucepan, melt butter and stir in brown sugar. Remove the pan from the heat and let it cool slightly. Whisk eggs and buttermilk into butter mixture until smooth and add to flour mixture, stirring very lightly until combined. Fold in chunks of apple. Divide batter into the muffin cups and bake for 15 minutes or until golden.

Heat ginger jelly in a small saucepan over low heat until just warm. Brush jam over muffins several times until absorbed for a nice glaze.

*For the longest shelf life, keep apples as cold as possible in the refrigerator. Apples won't freeze until the temperature sinks to 28.5° F.*

# Sunflower Granola

**Makes 12 cups**

The crisp, wholesome nature of granola reflects Washington's laid-back, outdoorsy lifestyle. What was once considered the epitome of "hippy food" in the 1960s and a snack food for hikers is now a mainstream breakfast item. A simple mixture of toasted whole grains, nuts and maple syrup (or honey), granola can be spruced up with dried Washington cranberries or cherries. It is best eaten with yogurt while wearing fuzzy slippers and poring over the *Sunday Times*.

**4 cups old-fashioned oats (not quick)**

**1 cup unsweetened, shredded coconut**

**1 cup dried fruit such as blueberries, cherries, sliced apricots**

**1 cup pumpkin seeds**

**1½ cups sunflower seeds**

**½ cup sesame seeds**

**1 cup wheat germ**

**1 cup chopped almonds**

**½ cup chopped cashews**

**⅔ cup maple syrup**

**1 tsp pure vanilla extract**

**½ tsp salt**

**¼ cup sunflower oil**

Preheat oven to 325° F. Place all ingredients in a large bowl and mix well. Spread on a baking sheet and bake for 15 minutes. Stir and bake 10 more minutes. Stir again and bake 5 to 10 minutes more until golden brown. Cool and store in an airtight container for up to a month.

**Tip**
Sprinkle granola over your favorite cereal or yogurt, or simply enjoy with milk. You can also eat it plain by the handful, or you can freeze it for use at another time.

# Sourdough Hotcakes

**Makes about 1 dozen**

The first leavened breads rose through the action of yeast naturally occurring on the grains and in the air. Before the advent of modern yeast packaging methods, people wanting to bake bread would keep a "starter" containing a proven yeast strain. Prospectors in the San Francisco Gold Rush discovered that their starters were unusually tangy, and the term "sourdough" was born. During a time when food was even more important than money, sourdough was extremely valuable to these prospectors; they used it to feed themselves and their dogs, and the starter was even used to tan hides. It is still popular as a leavening agent today, used by well-known bakeries such as the Essential Baking Company in Fremont and newcomer Bakery Nouveau in West Seattle.

### Quick Sourdough Starter

**1 cup water**

**1 cup unbleached flour**

**½ tsp active dry yeast**

### Sourdough Hotcakes

**2 cups sourdough starter (see above, opposite)**

**1½ cups unbleached or wholewheat flour**

**2 Tbsp sugar, maple syrup or honey**

**3 Tbsp canola oil**

**2 eggs**

**½ tsp sea salt**

**1 tsp baking powder**

**1 tsp baking soda, diluted in 1 Tbsp warm water**

The night before you plan to make hotcakes, mix starter ingredients well and set out on a countertop in a draft-free area, allowing the starter time to develop its characteristic sour taste. Remaining starter can be left on the counter for future use; it is best stored at 65 to 77° F. To strengthen and "feed" starter, add ¼ cup water and ½ cup flour every second day.

### Sourdough Hotcakes

Preheat griddle or pan to medium-high heat. Mix ingredients, except soda, together. Gently fold in soda and cook cakes right away so as to not lose the soda's leavening effect. Serve hot with your favorite condiments.

**Old-fashioned Sourdough Starter**
Boil unpeeled potatoes until they fall apart.
Remove skins. Mash potatoes in a nonmetallic
bowl, adding water as needed to make a rich, thick
liquid. Add remaining ingredients, beating until
smooth, and let stand for 1 week. Feed starter as
described opposite.

**2 large potatoes**

**3 Tbsp sugar**

**1⅔ cups unbleached flour**

**½ tsp active dry yeast**

# Cranberry Chutney

## Makes 4 cups

The word "cranberry" comes from "craneberry"; the flower looks like the head of a crane, and cranes were known to enjoy the berries. Cranberries were a vital food to Shoalwater Bay Indians and pioneers because of their naturally occurring benzoic acid, which is a great natural preservative, and their high vitamin C content. Although cranberries are thought of primarily as a Thanksgiving accompaniment, cranberry juice ranks third in sales in North America, after apple juice and orange juice. A large percentage of Washington's commercial cranberry crop (fifth in the nation in production) is grown in bogs on the Long Beach Peninsula. You can drive on the Cranberry Coast Scenic Byway through Washington's southwest coast and stop in at the Cranberry Museum in Long Beach.

1 Tbsp unsalted butter

8 oz pearl onions, peeled and left whole

2 Tbsp grated ginger

1 serrano chile, minced

2 kaffir lime leaves or 1 Tbsp lime zest

2¼ cups apple cider vinegar

1 cup light brown sugar

1 cup muscovado sugar

2 lbs fresh cranberries

¾ cup dried fruit such as currants, cranberries, blueberries or sour cherries

sea salt and freshly ground pepper

In a medium-sized pot, melt butter and sauté onions over medium heat for 5 minutes. Add next 6 ingredients and bring to a boil. Add cranberries and dried fruit, turn heat to medium-low and simmer for about 15 minutes or until chutney is thick and has reduced.

Season with salt and pepper, and refrigerate until well chilled.

### Tip
Instead of cranberries in this recipe, you could use rhubarb, apple, pear or peach—or experiment using a variety of fruits. You could also use cipollini, a small, flattened Italian variety of onion, instead of the pearl onions.

**Tip**
Pearl onions are more easily peeled if they are allowed
to sit in boiling hot water for a few minutes.

# Hazelnut Torte with Sour Cherry Preserve

## Serves 10 to 12

Hazelnuts originated in the Mediterranean, growing along the Black Sea around Turkey. Turkey still produces the majority of the world's hazelnuts, followed by Italy (Piedmont is reputed to have the best hazelnuts) and then the United States. Oregon is by far the largest producer of hazelnuts in the U.S. but there are also a handful of hazelnut producers here at home (see p. 128 for a reliable source.) As for preserves, you need look no further than Chukar Cherries, a Washington state institution found by Pam Montgomery 18 years ago. Based in Prosser, but with a Pike Place Market retail location (among others), Chukar Cherries are frequent carry-on companions to tourists taking back a slice of Washington state flavor to their families and friends. Look for Chukar Cherry Sour Cherry Preserve to accompany this torte.

2 cups cake flour

2 tsp baking powder

$1/2$ tsp salt

6 egg yolks

$1/2$ cup canola oil

$1/2$ cup water

1 cup sugar

6 egg whites

1 cup chopped, toasted hazelnuts (see p. 134)

$1/4$ cup strong brewed coffee, cooled

1 cup heavy cream (32 percent)

6 oz bittersweet chocolate, chopped

1 x 14 oz jar of Nutella chocolate hazelnut spread

toasted hazelnuts for garnish

1 x 8 oz jar of sour cherry preserve

Preheat oven to 350° F. Grease and lightly flour two 9-inch springform pans. Combine flour, baking powder and salt in a medium bowl and set aside. In a large mixing bowl, beat egg yolks, oil, water and sugar with an electric mixer on medium speed for 5 minutes, scraping bowl occasionally. Fold flour mixture into mixing bowl.

In another large mixing bowl, beat egg whites with an electric mixer on medium to high speed until soft peaks form. Gently fold about 1 cup of egg white mixture into the egg yolk mixture. Fold the rest of the egg yolk mixture into remaining egg white mixture. Then fold in the chopped hazelnuts. Spoon the batter evenly into prepared pans. Bake in oven for 20 minutes or until a toothpick inserted in the center comes out clean. Immediately poke holes all over the cakes with a toothpick and drizzle coffee evenly over. Let the cakes cool on wire racks for 10 minutes before removing from pans. When they have cooled completely, slice in half horizontally.

In a medium saucepan, heat cream to simmer. Remove from heat and add bittersweet chocolate, stirring until melted. Reserve ¼ cup of chocolate mixture for drizzling; cover and set aside. Cool remaining chocolate mixture to room temperature, about an hour. Transfer mixture to medium bowl and beat with an electric mixer on medium speed for 3 minutes or until it is thickened. Spread chocolate filling evenly on 3 cake layers, and frost the top and sides with chocolate hazelnut spread. Drizzle the reserved chocolate on top and garnish with toasted hazelnuts. Serve with sour cherry preserve on the side.

*For all types of nuts, a 3.5 oz serving has 550 to 700 calories and contains protein, phosphorus and potassium.*

# INDEX

# ABOUT THE AUTHORS

Becky Selengut is a private chef, cooking teacher and freelance writer who is proud to make Seattle, Washington her home. Selengut is the founder of www.SeasonalCornucopia.com, an educational website that celebrates the foods of the Pacific Northwest.

Jennifer Sayers Bajger is a chef and writer who has been cooking professionally for over 15 years— although she started in the kitchen long before that. She is passionate about fresh, local ingredients and believes that cooking and eating with the seasons enhances our enjoyment of food.

James Darcy brings a wealth of food experience to the table. He is a self-confessed epicure whose food and travel interests have taken him to tables around the world in France, Italy and Greece as well as Argentina and Borneo.

Chef Jennifer Ogle learned her craft from a variety of sources, among them the renowned French cooking school La Varenne. Today Jennifer co-owns a university-area bistro and enjoys all aspects of the culinary world.

# ABOUT THE PHOTOGRAPHER

Nanette Samol is a professional photographer who has been working in the industry for nearly 20 years. Her work has been published in various print media.